T0398656

GUARDIANS OF THE COMMUNITY

Guardians of the Community

The BLOCK PARENT® Program of Canada

KIMBERLY N. VARMA AND
KANWAL KHOKHAR

UNIVERSITY OF TORONTO PRESS
Toronto Buffalo London

© University of Toronto Press 2025
Toronto Buffalo London
utorontopress.com
Printed in Canada

ISBN 978-1-4875-6005-8 (cloth)   ISBN 978-1-4875-6007-2 (EPUB)
                                    ISBN 978-1-4875-6006-5 (PDF)

Library and Archives Canada Cataloguing in Publication

Title: Guardians of the community : the BLOCK PARENT® Program of
    Canada / Kimberly N. Varma and Kanwal Khokhar.
Names: Varma, Kimberly N., 1968– author | Khokhar, Kanwal, author.
Description: Includes bibliographical references and index.
Identifiers: Canadiana (print) 20240504488 | Canadiana (ebook)
    20240504100 | ISBN 9781487560058 (cloth) | ISBN 9781487560072 (EPUB) |
    ISBN 9781487560065 (PDF)
Subjects: LCSH: Block Parent Program of Canada – History. | LCSH:
    Community-based child welfare – Canada – History.
Classification: LCC HV745.A6 V37 2025 | DDC 362.70971 – dc23

Cover design: Sandra Friesen
Cover image: iStock.com / A-Digit

We wish to acknowledge the land on which the University of Toronto Press
operates. This land is the traditional territory of the Wendat, the Anishnaabeg,
the Haudenosaunee, the Métis, and the Mississaugas of the Credit First
Nation.

University of Toronto Press acknowledges the financial support of the
Government of Canada, the Canada Council for the Arts, and the Ontario Arts
Council, an agency of the Government of Ontario, for its publishing activities.

 Canada Council **Conseil des Arts**
for the Arts **du Canada**

Funded by the   Financé par le
Government   gouvernement
of Canada   du Canada

 Canada

ONTARIO ARTS COUNCIL
CONSEIL DES ARTS DE L'ONTARIO
an Ontario government agency
un organisme du gouvernement de l'Ontario

 MIX
Paper | Supporting
responsible forestry
FSC® C016245

In memory of my dad, J.P. Varma

Contents

Figures and Tables

Figures

Tables

Acknowledgments

This book would have not been possible without the valuable insights of those who dedicated themselves to the inception and continued administration of the Block Parent Program. We are indebted to so many people for being incredibly generous with their time and providing us with important perspectives on this program. Our gratitude goes out to George and Geri Jarvis, Marg Rooke, and Lynn Squance. We are especially grateful to Shelly Siskind and Arlene Gladstone for helping us understand the context that led to the inception of this program and for highlighting the work of so many dedicated women who established this national program that has continued for over five decades. We are also very fortunate to have been able to work alongside Jodi Lewchuk at the University of Toronto Press, who made this process incredibly smooth and uncomplicated for us. We are also greatly appreciative for the meticulous work of Perrin Lindelauf and to Leah Connor from the University of Toronto Press. We also owe a thank you to the anonymous reviewers and University of Toronto Press delegate for important suggestions that improved the manuscript greatly. Finally, we want to acknowledge the support and contribution of Linda Patterson, whom the first author contacted in 2018 to begin this study and who assisted us with this project up until publication of this book. We owe the utmost thanks to Linda, who devoted her time and energy to helping us understand this program, much in the way she has dedicated her time and energy to the Block Parent Program itself.

Kim Varma would like to thank I, J, CK, & P and the memory of S, for their patience and constant support. Thanks also to J&R, DV, & L, and especially to her mom for her unwavering and continual encouragement. She is also very fortunate to have worked with Kanwal Khokhar on this project from inception to conclusion and to share in the many roads that they travelled during this time.

Kanwal Khokhar would like to thank her husband Sheharyar for his love and reassurance, her family and mom for their encouragement and support, and Manahil Khokhar and Alexandra Polera for consistently cheering her on. And a special thank you to her dad, Fayyaz Khokhar, for his interest and enthusiasm in all her endeavours and for always giving her the safety and security to succeed in whatever she does. Additionally, a noteworthy thank you to Kimberly Varma for being a brilliant mentor and gracious co-author. Thank you.

GUARDIANS OF THE COMMUNITY

"Mothers on Watch"

On 9 February 1968, Canada's national newspaper ran a story about a developing conflict between mothers of school-aged children and the police in Etobicoke, Ontario, Canada. After a police commissioner fired the crossing guard assigned to the area near Rosethorn Public School, mothers of the students living in nearby Thorncrest Village began driving their children to school.

They were worried about the safety of their children as they walked to and from school. However, residents complained, and five mothers were ticketed while waiting to pick up their children in a no-parking zone. The local police maintained that they were obliged to ticket if they received complaints, but the mothers were steadfast intending to stand their ground and fight the $5 tickets in court as a collective. At stake was a non-negotiable situation – the safety of their children. "The police are usually so wonderful about safety" remarked one of the ticketed mothers. "I can't understand why they are after us for protecting our children."[1]

Tragically, on the very same day, approximately two hundred kilometres away in the southwestern Ontario city of London, nine-year-old Frankie Jensen left his home on Hazel Avenue at approximately 8:00 a.m. to make his way to Westdale Elementary School. Frankie never made it to school and his remains were found two months later. Though there is speculation about his likely killer, his case remains unsolved to this day.[2] In the weeks after Frankie's disappearance, the grim reality of his fate, as well as concerns about other alleged attacks on children, set off fears about the safety of children in London and the surrounding area, particularly for parents of young children (Arntfield, 2015). The panic that ensued in the London area in relation to the safety of children was intertwined with deep grief, sorrow, and outrage, and it became the main catalyst that mobilized the community towards the creation of a national child safety movement – the Block Parent Program of Canada.[3] The Program started in London, Ontario, in 1968 and was Canada's largest volunteer-run child safety program. The approach taken was that refuge for children who needed protection could be found in every neighbourhood and community across the country. Volunteer "Block Parents" (predominantly homemakers and mothers of small children) would place signs in their front windows to indicate they were available to provide a safe refuge for children who needed help. To this end, safety and assistance could be found in these designated homes for children or other community members who were in distress. In addition to providing a safe haven, the program's signage was thought to deter possible predators from preying on children thus preventing crime in the community.

The Program started shortly after the tragic case of Frankie Jensen. As observed by one of the founders of the program, "the community was outraged, the family was grieving and the question was, how did this happen?" Unfortunately, the tragedy that occurred in Frankie Jensen's case would repeat over and over again in communities across Canada in the decades that followed, activating community participation for greater child protection.

Guardians of the Community

Responses to the spectrum of concerns for children's welfare – child safety, child protection, and even child delinquency – have taken a variety of forms in Canada and other Western democracies over the past century with guardianship as a central focus. The emphasis on childhood as a distinct area of enquiry that informed institutionalized responses to appropriate child-rearing and guardianship was influenced by a nineteenth century psychologist, G. Stanley Hall, whose interests centred on child development and evolutionary theory. While Hall's theories were met with controversy by academics at the time, his work garnered a popular following and influenced how motherhood and child caregiving was to be organized. So-called mother's clubs and child-study groups became venues open to the public where Hall's ideas about the nature of childhood along with practical training and instruction for caregiving mothers on the stages of child development were promoted (Young, 2016, p. 203).

Hall's work highlighted the importance of maternal caregiving for child-rearing and child protection, and the late nineteenth and early twentieth centuries witnessed the arrival of even more institutionalized responses to child protection and governance, in the form of private, charitable, religious, and philanthropic organizations along with institutionalized, state-sponsored programming for child protection. The "child saving" movement of the twentieth century led by social reformers sought to protect children from the physical and moral dangers of urban society (Platt, 1977, p. 4) and resulted in the creation of institutions for neglected, abused, and destitute youth, as these social issues were thought to lead to juvenile delinquency. The creation of the first Children's Aid Society in 1891 and the passage of the first child protection legislation only two years later solidified state responses to the plight of children and youth. Though as pointed out by Platt and others, while intentions were benevolent, the end result was the creation of institutions that created more harm than good (Platt, 1977; Rothman, 1980).

The range of institutionalized responses to the welfare and protection of children, alongside delinquency, viewed children and adolescents as both "a risk" and "at risk," meaning that there was little distinction between neglected and delinquent youth "since the former were but incipient versions of the latter" (Fox, 1984, p. 152). Therefore, the idea that one could protect society through protecting children became a central feature of debates preceding the passing of the first youth justice legislation in Canada, the Juvenile Delinquents Act of 1908 (Trépanier, 1999).

The Juvenile Delinquents Act reflected the view that youth who were neglected, abused, or who committed offences needed protection, guidance, and assistance by the state, which came in the form of *parens patriae* – the state adopting a parental role to provide help and safety to youth. This concept of the state as guardian of the community can be seen in early discussions about the state's role in juvenile justice legislation. The state theoretically represented, as closely as possible, the relationship between parent and child (Rothman, 1980; Simon, 1995; Chunn, 1992). Moreover, early juvenile justice structures and workers of the court reproduced, as closely as possible, what they considered to be good parenting and a sound upbringing though, as noted by Iacovetta (1999, p. 597), post-war suburban court workers ended up reinforcing middle-class and Eurocentric codes of conduct, including middle-class family values, which were not always reflective of the families that found themselves in juvenile court settings. As also pointed out by historians, early juvenile courts were a site of contestation between youth, parents, court workers, and judges. Myers's (2021) examination of "delinquent daughters" in Montreal's juvenile courts in the early twentieth century revealed that the juvenile court provided an extension of maternal rule into the larger life of the community through the appointment of women to judicial and other criminal justice roles, allowing them to maintain their domain over matters of children and family life (Myers, 2021, p. 679).

Overall, the ethos behind early juvenile justice institutions was that the state could act as guardian of the community, and in the late nineteenth century there was an assumption that the protection of children translated to the protection of society. To this end, industrial and reform schools provided children who were potential victims or delinquents a safe refuge.[4]

Safe Refuge within Communities, Maternal Guardianship, and Building Solidarity

State guardianship, as noted above, viewed children as all in "need of protection," with the judge serving as "father of the country." However, in the 1960s guardianship in the community for the protection of children was led by a different kind of guardian. In the tragic case of Frankie Jensen and regarding the safety concerns for the mothers of Thorncrest Village in 1968, the protection of their children could not solely be addressed by the police, giving rise to a different kind of parental governance – that of *maternal guardianship* and community involvement in the prevention of crime.

The communities' involvement in crime prevention was relatively new. Prior to the 1960s, crime prevention in most communities was solely within the purview of the police. In the mid-1960s, communities were given a greater role in preventing crime, but it was still a passive role as the "eyes and ears" of police. In the early 1970s, while communities were still on the sidelines, the emphasis of crime prevention initiatives centred on the protection of children and youth (Vallée, 2010). It was during this time that the birth of a program – Block Parent – with a unique model of maternal guardianship would significantly change the crime prevention and child protection landscape in Canada.

The inception and mobilization of the Block Parent Program can be understood within a broader theoretical context that considers community crime prevention and child protection programs as a means of creating and reinforcing social solidarity, particularly in view of perceived social instability and moral panic. As argued by Durkheim (1912/1986), a common purpose, and the rituals that communities[5] engage in around that purpose, redefines and reinforces a collective consciousness, further binding members of that community together. These customs, along with the strategies to deal with preventing crime, are more than instrumental, they are symbolic statements about the way society sees its present, past, and future (Sutton et al., 2021, p. 137). For Block

Parent, the focus on child protection solidified the communities' affirmation of child safety in light of the tragic case of Frankie Jensen, as well as reaffirming the traditional role of family, maternal childcare, and protection. This was particularly salient due to post-war anxieties surrounding the corruption of youth, as well as fears about the stability of the nuclear family as women began to enter the workforce. For example, during the 1950s, there were concerted efforts to address the indecency of crime comics and objectionable literature as corrupting influences on youth (Adams, 1995; O'Malley, 2023); there was moral panic about the apparent widespread use of drugs by Toronto adolescents between 1945 and 1960 despite evidence to the contrary (Karibo, 2008); and there were reports of notorious inner-city neighbourhoods as inherently deviant spaces that corrupted children in the Toronto area (Iacovetta, 1999). At a time when there was a great deal of anxiety about the corruption of youth, fears about child molesters, and a lack of maternal supervision, Block Parent provided stability and strength – neighbourhood by neighbourhood, As noted by Constable Henry Huizinga in a 1976 edition of *Homemakers* magazine, when a community joined the Block Parent Program, it meant that child sexual predators "were forced to find a safer hunting ground" (Morris, 1976, p. 20). The displacement of child sexual predators to another community safeguarded each community on "watch" and this, in turn, reinforced morals, values, and civic duty to children in that community, despite evidence that children and youth were more at risk from domestic abuse or violence in the home than they were from "stranger danger" (Heidinger, 2022). The same concerns surrounding community cohesion, moral panic about child sexual predators, and displacement can be seen in the United States. As discussed by Durling (2006), the fear of sex offenders has resulted in registries and residency restrictions, which are not only unconstitutional, but also do not keep children or others who may be vulnerable safe. The perceived risk does not match the empirical data on child safety risks.

Even though the actual risks of stranger danger were low, Block Parent emerged at a time when "something had to be done" in the London community, and while centred on child safety, the program symbolized something more. What Block Parent represented on a smaller scale was community solidarity through the rituals and everyday exchanges between members (Goffman, 1959). Ritual theory revolves around meaning – the forces that compel members of a society to engage in activities that foster social and emotional solidarity despite their differences (Rossner & Meher, 2014, p. 200). Ritual occurs through repeated social interactions surrounding meaning or purpose. In the case of Block Parent, that purpose was community, child safety, maternal governance, and the solidification of the family unit. These rituals and repeated social interactions around purpose or meaning have to be continually fostered and must be intentional. As noted by David Garland, in large, complex societies, social bonding and solidarity do not happen organically outside of families and small groups but instead have to be built in order to create opportunities for routine practices of mutual aid, shared citizenship, and a "fellow feeling" (Garland, 2023, p. 57). Forty years ago, Canada's solicitor general reminded Canadian citizens of this purpose, that good neighbours look out for each other. "Part of being a good neighbour means keeping a friendly eye out for each other, or being alert to occasions when help might be needed" (Minister of Supply and Services, Canada, 1983). Thus, in the absence of mutual aid and shared citizenship as might be found in small groups or families, the intentional building of communities with purpose must be created, as was the case with Block Parent.

Scholars have noted the importance of rituals of reintegrative shaming, reconciliation, and redemption (Rossner, 2019) as mechanisms to affirm community morals, values, purpose, and a sense of shared citizenship (Braithwaite, 2000; Rossner, 2019). For the Block Parent Program, and from the lens of community crime prevention, the rituals of engagement consisted of joining in a shared responsibility for child protection by volunteering and serving as a guardian; placing a sign in the window to indicate that "this house is open" for children who need help; providing teachers with educational materials and training for school-aged children; and partnering with local police and local businesses for support. All of these practices provided an organized sense of identity and shared citizenship, and they reaffirmed and reproduced community solidarity around the project of child protection.

Moreover, Block Parent tapped into an emotional and instrumental facet of community crime prevention. As Freiberg notes, crime prevention strategies can only be successful if they are able to address the "deep-seated psychological and affective needs" of the public, and they must incorporate instrumental responses, address emotional needs, and produce social cohesion (Freiberg, 2001, p. 265). Block Parent was conceived of and executed shortly after the tragic abduction and murder of a young boy on his way to school. The community grief over this loss, along with the ensuing fear for the safety of children in the area, addressed the need to "do something." Thus, the devastated London community in 1968 did something by creating a program centring on maternal guardianship and safe havens (instrumental), addressing the fear for the safety of other children (emotional), and banding the community together to create social cohesion. The Block Parent Program created this ethos in the community, partnering with schools, and with the assistance of the local police under the umbrella and common purpose of child protection which served both instrumental and symbolic purposes (Sutton et al., 2021).

It is also interesting to note that during this time in the late 1960s, community members (mothers and predominantly women homemakers) led the charge (not governments or the police) to mobilize around community child protection, and they did so rapidly. This social movement was purposeful, organized, and strived towards a common goal, and it resulted in the largest volunteer-run child safety and crime prevention program in Canada, lasting half a century and still continuing today in some smaller jurisdictions. Many questions arise in attempting to understand this particular social movement. How did the circumstances allow for rapid deployment and buy-in from police and school agencies? Under which circumstances do members of a community mobilize for the purposes of crime prevention and in what kinds of conditions (Schneider, 2007)? Why did this program succeed so quickly and what caused the decline? Finally, is there a role for community in crime prevention and child safety in the current context?

Aim and Scope of the Book

The purpose of this book is to examine the social, political, technological, and cultural conditions that initiated the Block Parent Program and to understand how the landscape of child protection and community crime prevention has shifted over the last five decades. This book draws upon open-ended interviews with key sources, stakeholders, and those who introduced the Block Parent Program; annual reports, memos, minutes of meetings, and other documents from the Block Parent National Program; Hansard debates, social media, and newspaper sources; and a survey of almost 1,300 Canadians on crime prevention, neighbourhood safety, and child safety concerns conducted in the summer of 2021. Our interest is in the interaction between community engagement, civic responsibility, and concerns around child protection along with exploration of the motivations underlying involvement in community safety programs such as fear of crime, community cohesion, police confidence, and perceptions of child safety.

This book outlines the Block Parent Program's inception and decline over five decades, which serves as a microcosm for significant changes that occurred in family and economic structure over this period. These general themes – routine activities theories and women as volunteer guardians, women entering the workforce, concerns about "latchkey" kids, child protection and "stranger danger," community cohesion and solidarity, and changes in technology including social media and online crime prevention applications – will be traced throughout the book. We also conclude our analysis by exploring the program from a community health and wellness perspective. While the foundations of the program have shifted quite considerably in the last five decades, examining what "Guardians of the Community" might look like today is important to contemplate. Addressing a lack of community cohesion, assisting people in need or who are isolated, addressing fear of crime, and creating the conditions for increased community mobilization might well be a new way of repurposing a Block Parent approach.

Chapter 1, entitled "A Refuge for Children from the City Jungles of North America," examines the inception of the Block Parent Program in Canada, from the tragic abduction and murder of Frankie Jensen to the rapid rise of the program. The conditions for community mobilization lined up precisely in that moment of grief and gave rise to an innovative program, which was, in part, based on shifting theories of crime. For example, rather than focusing solely on the motivation of the offender or the vulnerability of the victim, opportunity theories of crime such as situational crime prevention highlighted the way in which chances for crime are reduced by increasing risks and reducing rewards of crime within a situational context.

Opportunity theories built on principles of Social Disorganization theory (Shaw & McKay, 1942) which focused on "place" – how neighbourhoods may create the conditions that are favourable (or unfavourable) to crime (Kubrin et al., 2021). Thus, strengthening networks of informal and formal social control and increasing community solidarity were important factors in preventing crime and disorder (Cohen & Felson, 1979; Brantingham & Brantingham, 1993; Sampson et al., 1997). In addition, the responsibilization strategy of communities working in partnership with law enforcement authorities in order to prevent and control crime was central to this shift (O'Malley & Palmer, 1996; Garland, 2001; Johnston & Shearing, 2002). As indicated by Hunter (1985, p. 239), the success of local crime control programs is dependent upon being embedded in ongoing community organizations. Voluntary recruitment and sustained participation work in interlock with local institutions – religious organizations, schools, and local businesses contribute to overall programming. This interdependence was at the very heart of the Block Parent model.

Another important theory of crime prevention circulating at the time was routine activities theory and the notion of capable guardianship

(Cohen & Felson, 1979). The value of maternal guardianship was a key aspect of Block Parent in that protection came from mostly women volunteers who were not yet in the workforce; however, this was a time when women were beginning to expand their personal and professional roles in society. The 1960s onwards was characterized with (mostly) women who stayed at home, many of whom were caring for children, but in the late 1960s and early 1970s, women entered the workforce and were involved in the community in a more professional capacity. However, with women working outside of the home, another child safety concern arose about so-called latchkey children who returned from school to an empty home and spent large portions of their time unsupervised until a parent returned home after the workday. This lack of at-home guardianship has persisted. Most people continue to work outside of the home,[6] and when it comes to child protection and guardianship, being driven to and from school is more common than walking, many carry cell phones for safety (in addition to other features such as GPS tracking), and Amber Alerts have become the mechanisms by which the public is alerted in cases of child abduction. Thus, the last fifty years have seen a shift from homemakers providing guardianship to technological modes of guardianship.

Chapter 2, "The Rise and Fall of the Block Parent Program," traces the rapid growth and decline of Block Parent. In addition to focusing on child protection and guardianship, this book chronicles the conditions that enabled the growth of community mobilization at the grassroots level, which was in response to fear, loss, and grief. This analysis is unique in that child protection within the realm of community mobilization has not been fully understood. While there has been a great deal of research on Neighbourhood Watch or other cognate programs, Block Parent is distinct in that it centres on guardianship and human interaction. Research suggests that guardianship as a construct has to include "capability," which relates to the willingness to supervise, the ability to detect, and the willingness to intervene (Reynald, 2010; Van Bavel, 2019; Hollis et al., 2019). The Block Parent model provided all of these elements in that capable guardians (predominantly homemakers) were willing (placing a sign in their window) and would supervise, detect, and intervene (in opening their home to a child in need).

In tracing the ebbs and flows of the Block Parent Program, this chapter illustrates that tragic incidents involving children became the catalysts for renewed calls for community safety programs focused on child protection. Block Parent also became associated with a certain kind of prestige for women as volunteers as they were exploring their potential as professionals in the community. This was illustrated when the then governor general's wife, Lily Schreyer, flew the Block Parent flag high over Rideau Hall in 1981, signifying a greater status for women as having a more professional role but still within traditional confines of caregiving and child protection.

The upward momentum of the program was significant with the rapid increase of volunteer homes and greater media attention across the country. The seamless integration between community, schools, and local police was notable, and the training materials provided to educators and volunteers was well organized. While records were kept on the number of "knocks at the door" and the reason for the distress through incident reports that had to be completed by volunteers every time a child used a Block Parent home, the records were not particularly rigorous (Block Parent Program of Canada, 1990, p. 2), which speaks to a movement that was truly grassroots and informal – though formalized. The program extended outwards to local businesses that acted as Block Parent businesses and that provided small amounts of funding, in addition to the provincial and federal grants that sustained the program along with fundraising efforts. Block Parent volunteers even organized "lost children booths" at fairs and festivals, reuniting lost children with their parents (Block Parent Program of Canada, 2009).

The latter half of the chapter examines the decline of the program due to a lack of volunteers (in part attributed to women entering the workforce in greater numbers), enhanced police checks for individuals in the homes of volunteers, and the greater use of technology including mobile phones as a way to provide security for children outside of the home.

Significantly, concerns about safety and accountability became directed at the Block Parent sign itself, with fears that child molesters would access the signs to lure children. This concern led to a decline in police support and had a dramatic effect on the viability of the program. The impetus for the inception of the Block Parent Program – worries about child predators after the tragedy in London – was the very same concern that was a factor in ending the program, the potential for the misuse of signs by child molesters.

While the decline in Block Parent has been significant, there have been calls for its revival. Chapter 3, "The Fate of Block Parent: Adaptation and Relevance," examines the way in which programs such as Block Parent fulfil a societal role for child safety and beyond. The research presented in the book shows that community solidarity is cultivated through these programs and that neighbourhood cohesion and civic engagement, which are fostered through programs like Block Parent, have positive effects on health and well-being (Toronto, 2022; Pinker, 2014; Bjornstrom, 2011). We present research from a survey of almost

1,300 Canadians in July and August 2021 examining volunteerism, civic responsibility, concerns around child protection, and perceptions of the purpose of Block Parent types of program in relation to community safety. Results show that "knowing one's neighbours" appears to be a very important factor in determining whether to participate in-person as a volunteer, suggesting that community solidarity is at the heart of this program.

In chapter 4, "Communities, Collective Consciousness, and Protection for Vulnerable Populations," we examine the nature and extent of the Block Parent Program in terms of the incidents and reporting of activities that provided empirical evidence of their work, as well as symbolic confirmation of the Block Parent ethos. This chapter examines the powerful nature of perceptions – "stranger danger" in relation to the protection of youth, a belief in deterrence as emanating from guardians on watch and through signage, and the desire for community cohesion – as providing the foundation for this program, which gained enormous traction in a very short period. Our analysis breaks new ground by discussing crime prevention through the unique concerns of child protection and community mobilization from both an instrumental and symbolic perspective.

We also examine the way in which community grief fuels and feeds such a movement. We end with a discussion of what Block Parent means in the current context. Why do some people harken back to a time when Block Parent was pervasive? How has Block Parent adapted to the changes in stay-at-home guardianship, technology, diversity, and community cohesion? When a community is grieving, how is healing mobilized? What about marginalized communities that lack the community or social capital to protect youth? How do we reconcile domestic violence and child abuse in terms of the risk to children and youth? In the current context, who are the active citizens attempting to address these issues and how do they go about enacting change?

We conclude by examining the Block Parent Program as a microcosm for five decades of change in society – the rapid changes that saw women working outside of the home, a greater use of technology, more supervised child mobility and "helicopter parenting," and concerns about strangers and child molesters. Block Parent provided a perception of stability of family and community in a period of flux. What has stayed the same in today's context is a need for community and a sense of belonging. What has changed is a recognition that child protection needs to be viewed more broadly, but also that a perception of safety goes a long way for community well-being. To this end, this research advances our knowledge of community mobilization on social issues such as child protection, or more broadly, guardianship for other vulnerable populations. It contributes to our understanding of civic responsibility and its relationship to child protection concerns. This work also provides insight into the dynamics of community mobilization, guardianship, the conditions that spark the need to organize, and the challenges facing communities that are grieving.

Our analysis will be of interest to those working in the areas of criminology, public policy and community engagement, child welfare, and policing and crime prevention. Most importantly, this work will be of use for communities themselves who are interested in engaging in crime prevention, creating safe spaces for children in their homes and their communities, and assisting others in need. Understanding the challenges of diversity in communities, issues of civic responsibility, volunteerism and time commitment, and social media and other forms of crime prevention engagement will be of value to communities who wish to contribute to the safety of their residents.

Chapter 1

"A Refuge for Children from the City Jungles of North America"

The London Chapter of the National Council of Jewish Women (NCJW) became the catalyst that brought about the original inception of the Block Parent Program of Canada. The NCJW was a progressive organization that addressed social issues through advocacy, education, and social action. Eight months after Frankie Jensen went missing, the Public Affairs Study Group of the NCJW, London Chapter, organized a meeting that included highly motivated young mothers, their infants in tow, who were concerned about the safety of children in the area. The London community was outraged, the Jensen family was grieving, and the NCJW began to mobilize.

A member of the NCJW Public Affairs Study Group, Ellen Brownstone, was instrumental in bringing forward information to the initial meeting of the Study Group indicating that the London Police were seeking a partnership to implement a program targeting child safety. The general concept of Block Parent was traced back to London, England, during World War II (Block Parent Program of Canada, 1990, p. 3) and the London, Ontario, local police were aware of a few small-scale crime prevention programs running in moderate-sized communities in New York, parts of California, and Nebraska in the early 1960s, which they provided as potential models (see figure 1 showing an American Block Parent sign). In the minutes of a meeting held on 15 October 1968 by the Public Affairs Study Group of the NCJW, the aims and mandate of the NCJW and concerns about the Jensen case were discussed.

Following this, Superintendent Len Elgie of the London Police Force provided statistics from 1967 on child molestations in the London area, noting there were ninety-two victims under the age of sixteen molested by seventy-one offenders ranging in age between five and seventy-eight years (Minutes, NCJW, October 1968). This, of course, reinforced the fears and worries of residents living in the London community. The tragedy of Frankie Jensen, along with the statistics presented, heightened the urgency to act quickly towards an organized child safety program in the London community.

Two US programs were highlighted by the NCJW as potential contenders to address the desperate need for child protection in London, Ontario. One program, from Niagara Falls, New York, which started in 1967, was focused on deterring "troublemakers" from entering school districts. This program was roughly based on those running in St. Louis, Missouri; Virginia Beach, Virginia; and most notably Erie, Pennsylvania. It was the first of its kind in New York State and was conceived to address a range of community safety concerns, creating a "refuge for children in the city jungles of North America – not only from perverts, but in the event of accidents or illness."[1] Women volunteers from "all walks of life – wives of policemen, plumbers and construction workers" served as volunteers, including a Canadian woman, Mrs. Edward Marcolini, who was profiled in the *Globe and Mail* as the first volunteer for this program. As discussed by Captain Joseph Conti, head of the Niagara Falls, New York, Police Department's community service unit, in the first month after the operation of Block Parent, none of the 145 volunteer mothers had to deal with an incident. "We feel that the success of the program will be if the Block Parents don't have to do anything. Just the fact that they exist is a comfort to us in the police department and should be for the parents." It is interesting to note that, even early on, the program allure was based on the perception of safety offered versus actual intervention in incidents.

Another program, out of Port Hueneme, California, was similar but had the added benefit of greater community involvement instead of sole reliance on the police (NCJW minutes of meeting 15 October 1968). The "Helping Hands" program from Port Hueneme started in 1965 by two women from the Parkview School Parent Teachers Association, Mrs. Boatright and Mrs. Pope, who modelled Port Hueneme on information they received about a Block Parent Program running in Omaha, Nebraska (Minutes, NCJW October 1968). According to Police Chief Al Jalaty, the Port Hueneme program was estimated to reduce child molestations by 90 per cent. The program was not a "police program, but a *parent* program (our emphasis)." Chief Jalaty also noted the added benefit that "it has also brought the people closer to law enforcement ... They have become a part of the police department through their cooperation" (Congressional Record, 1967). Chief Jalaty sent information on the Port Hueneme Block Parent Program to Walter Johnson, acting chief of police for London, Ontario, in April of 1968, highlighting the benefits of the Port Hueneme program. From there, the NCJW of London adopted a mixture of the New York and Port Hueneme models and mobilized the

The sign on the left is the American Block Parent sign as used in the 1960's in towns such as Omaha, Nebraska, Niagara Falls, New York and Port Hueneme, California

Figure 1. American Block Parent Sign.
Source: Block Parent Program of Canada, 1991.

support of London area police and two London school boards to start a Block Parent pilot project in five elementary schools in the fall of 1968. Two years after the pilot projects were created, in 1970, all London elementary schools had adopted Block Parent and the results were clear – police in the area noticed a deterrent effect – a drop in child-related and overall crimes and a concomitant "displacement" effect where surrounding jurisdictions had increased crime rates. The London Police attributed this decline in the crime rate to the deterrent impact of the Block Parent signs (Block Parent Program of Canada, 1990, p. 3).

The Block Parent Program quickly spread to surrounding areas – St. Thomas, Sarnia, Hamilton, and Ottawa; in 1973 the first Block Parent Program opened outside of the province of Ontario, in Edmonton, Alberta. In 1975 the Canadian Safety Council promoted the Block Parent Program using London as the model and in 1976, after *Homemakers* magazine ran a "call to action" to adopt the Block Parent Program, it quickly spread to communities across Canada. In May 1977, the first Block Parent conference was held in London, Ontario, and the first provincial Block Parent Program was formed in Ontario. Less than twenty years later the Block Parent Program became national and at its height had over 500,000 participating homes to protect Canadian children (Block Parent Program of Canada, 1990).

The Emergence of Block Parent – Fear, Deterrence, and Displacement

Concerns about child safety, whether due to traffic, bullying, lost children, or stranger danger, have been central features of crime control initiatives for decades. The difference in the late 1960s was that the Block Parent Program was seen as a unique and innovative way of addressing child protection concerns for two main reasons. First, the program was contextualized as able "do everything" from providing refuge to children who were feared to be targeted by strangers to providing a child with cursory medical assistance. For example, as noted by Toronto Controller Frederick Beavis, a Block Parent Program "could cut down on molesting and purse-snatchings" and "could also help diabetics."[2] The Block Parent Program was envisioned as a way to prevent a very broad spectrum of crime and disorder issues with a specific focus on child protection. Not only was there a belief in a deterrent impact of warning away would-be child molesters, but the program offered a safe haven for children who might have a physical injury, were lost, were being bullied, or even being chased by a dog.

Second, while the deterrent value of the program was implied, the structure of the program aligned well with a major theory of crime that was proposed in the late 1970s. Cohen and Felson's (1979) "routine activities theory" moved the emphasis of criminological research away from explanations examining the characteristic of offenders who commit crimes and towards an understanding of the circumstances that give rise to predatory street crime, also known as situational crime prevention. Routine activities theory posits that for a crime to occur, there has to be the coming together in time and place of three elements: a motivated offender, a suitable target, and the absence of a capable guardian. While the first two elements (motivated offender and suitable target) were more difficult to address, guardianship could be aptly solved through the Block Parent Program. Children who were in distress due to a stranger or bully would be provided a capable guardian through the Block Parent Program in the form of women who were mostly at home and constituted the volunteer workforce behind this program. *Safe Havens* in the form of houses provided shelter and were located in communities and neighbourhoods across Canada, allowing guardianship and protective shelter to be *anywhere and everywhere*. Moreover, the deterrent impact of Block Parent signs and "women on watch" would displace crime to other communities – an incentive for all communities to sign on. Carol Bladon, the chairperson of the London Block Parent Centre Committee, stated that the signs acted as a deterrent and a "silent warning" that told would-be offenders to "stay out of this neighbourhood, we are protecting our young!" (Morris, 1976, p. 8). The belief in the deterrent effect of the program was also potent. According to Constable Henry Huizinga from the London Police Department, the signs are similar to when a police cruiser is coming up behind a vehicle: "you slow down whether you have been speeding or not, you're going to be more careful. They're not going to park in a block

Figure 2. Officially a Block Parent Community – St. Thomas, Ontario, 1980.
It's Official – The St. Thomas Block Parent Association erected signs at the east
and west ends of Talbot Street Saturday officially recognizing St. Thomas as a
Block Parent community. Helping to erect one of the signs near First Avenue
are, from left, Art Shores, Bob Ranson, Jim Murray, and Bill Bow, while Steven
Shores, 4, gives moral support.
Source: Elgin County Archives, *St. Thomas Times Journal*, 12 May 1980.

where there is a sign – they go somewhere else. This is where the Block
Parent organization, with that sign, is most effective" (Morris, 1976, p.
20). The displacement of crime and disorder to neighbouring communities was part of the reason for the surge of Block Parent communities.
If every neighbourhood had Block Parents, there would be nowhere for
potential offenders to go. As figure 2 shows, raising the sign was part of
the symbolism for the protection of the community.

While there was unified interest in Block Parent and the rapid buy-in
from schools and police departments, there were some that felt that
informal community social networks were sufficient for the protection
of children. A month after Beavis's call to examine the Block Parent

plan in 1968, the Scarborough council decided there was no need for this program in their jurisdiction because this was already unofficially occurring courtesy of local neighbourhood parents. As stated by the mayor, Albert Campbell, "Scarboro [*sic*] children can run to any home in an emergency"; furthermore, as discussed by Scarborough controller Karl Mallette, "child molesting in Scarboro [*sic*] is not nearly what it is in the United States."[3]

Despite the informal networks already in place in Scarborough and quite likely in Toronto and other metropolitan areas, in 1968 the Block Parent Program did indeed become a national volunteer-run program in Canada, which had at its core the Block Parent home as a place of refuge.

Women as Mobilizers

The role of the community in neighbourhood crime prevention has varied over the decades. According to Vallée's (2010) historical overview of a century of crime prevention efforts in Canada, from the late nineteenth century to the 1960s, crime prevention was primarily spearheaded by policing agencies, most notably the RCMP, with little community engagement. It was only in the mid-1960s that the role of community was given attention, and in the early 1970s there was an emphasis on crime prevention initiatives involving children and youth. It was not until the early 1980s that academics and practitioners both became involved in a more sustained way in crime prevention initiatives, specifically through community social development. With the inception of the National Crime Prevention Council (NCPC) in 1994, more stable and organized funding for crime prevention initiatives occurred along with the NCPC taking on an additional role of providing advice to governments on proactive approaches to addressing crime, victimization, and insecurity. In addition the NCPC provided a voice for the community in the development of crime prevention policy (Vallée, 2010; Hastings, 2005).

What was unique about the Block Parent Program was that its key volunteers, administrators, and marketers were mostly women. This was during the second wave of feminism in which assumptions about the conventional roles of women in society and in the family were being widely questioned. Pat Cooper, writing for the journal *Atlantis*, noted that the new era for women was one in which they were no longer located within the "triangle of children, husband and home" (Cooper, 1979, p. 123), but rather the world was opening up for all women, including those that lacked professional degrees or experience in the labour market. For Cooper, it was important that women used their power to promote social change and influence public policy, first by educating members about the needs of the community, and second by lobbying decision-makers on gaps in services to the community (Cooper, 1979, p. 14). This vision translated directly to the work carried out by the Public Affairs Committee of the NCJW, comprised mainly of five women – Shelly Siskind, Arlene Gropper (now, Arlene Gladstone), Ellen Rosen, Sharon Richmond, and Gerbrig Berman, and other women such as Sandi Caplan, who continued this work and later initiated a program called Heart to Heart under the NCJW umbrella.[4] This committee was tasked with seeking out community gaps and mobilizing around community needs. The NCJW had a long legacy of women who were trail-blazers, particularly at this time in the 1960s, when social clubs were the exclusive territory of the elite and were noticeably lacking in (racial and gender) diversity. The leadership from these women – Phyllis Cohen, a business woman who worked alongside her husband and established the Central Volunteer Bureau through the NCJW; and Eva Goldenberg, a widow and mother who came to London to work as executive director of the London Jewish Community Centre and became a mentor to many women in the community – preceded the young mothers of the Public Affairs Committee who mobilized Block Parent. This group of women mentors were "educated, privileged, powerful women in their own rights, still homemakers – didn't go out to work outside the home – but had the idea that this organization [the NCJW] ... dedicates itself to the good of the entire Canadian community, not necessarily just the Jewish community, and it's in a way, a statement of belonging and respect for our various identities." As mentioned above, a key driver of the program was NCJW member Ellen Brownstone. An orphan survivor of the Holocaust, Brownstone was dedicated to saving the lives of children. She worked as a kindergarten teacher, and similar to many of the other members of the NCJW, was a mother of young children. Like many in the small community of London, Ontario, she knew the Jensen family and had heard of a community child safety program akin to what became Block Parent. She brought the issue to the attention of the Public Affairs Committee. From here, the young mothers of the NCJW took up the charge. They were out at least three nights per week, along with the police, discussing the logistics of the program, going to school counsel meetings, and providing the information, sales, and marketing for the program for parents of school-aged children.

Working with schools (both public and Catholic schools) was an important aspect of moving the program forward. In order to create awareness among children in local elementary schools, presentations were conducted during evening parent-school counsel meetings. While fears about child safety were already high among parents of school-aged children in the London area, the school presentations would further set the stage for mobilization with fear of child molesters as a driver. Presentations would be introduced with a film called the "Child Molester" screened by the owner of the local funeral home. Once the film was finished, the members from the NCJW Block Parent Program were introduced along with the "morality squad" of the London Police Force.[5] Parents and community members would be provided with a description of the program and how it might protect their children as well as how to get involved. At one of the school meetings, a father of one of the students introduced himself to a few of the NCJW members indicating that he worked for Labatt Brewing and wanted to assist with the program. He invited two of the members of the NCJW Public Affairs Study Group to a meeting at Labatt's office and showed them a mock-up of a possible sign created by their marketing department. The original sign provided by Labatt (see figure 3) is still in use and is most recognizable today.

There were four basic needs that the founders of Block Parent wanted to have in place for the purposes of protecting children and vulnerable adults in the community: "safe spaces" on every block where children could run for help in an emergency; education about strangers, the dangers of society, and how to use the Block Parent Program; early warning systems between the school and the home in case the child did not arrive; and an organized telephone network between police and the public to search for a missing child or adult (Block Parent Program of Canada, 1990, p. 3). A number of these initiatives remain in place today, such as school attendance phone calls.

The advocacy by the women of the NCJW set the stage for Block Parent in London and surrounding areas in the early to mid-1970s, and all of the conditions and partnerships seemed to fall into place seamlessly. Part of this was the timing, and the other aspect was that many people knew each other, and the population of London was not too large (237,000 in 1968).[6] Most residents knew the Jensen family as they ran the local furniture store. The young mothers of the NCJW simply made calls to people who could help, and most were willing to get involved.

By the fall of 1970, the Block Parent Program was running in almost all of London's schools, including both school boards, and began to spread quickly into surrounding areas in the early 1970s. In the initial stages of the program, a prospective volunteer would fill out an application, anyone over the age of eighteen in the home would be screened by police (free of charge), and they would be given a sign for their window. As pointed out in the 1990 Annual Report, these volunteers were "ordinary" people who had volunteered to act as responsible adults in emergency situations

Figure 3. Block Parent Program Sign, Canada. A red and white background and a drawing of a young boy holding the hand of an adult woman wearing a skirt. Labatt provided their services for the sign gratuitously and did not seek out any publicity associated with this work.
Source: Block Parent Program of Canada.

for the residents in their community and moreover were considered *safe strangers*[7] because they were screened by police.

Eight years after the program started, a "call to action" in a 1976 issue of *Homemakers* magazine called "Protecting the Kids in your Neighbourhood" had a profound influence on the proliferation of the Block Parent Program across Canada. Speaking to the readership of *Homemakers*, author Eileen Morris advocated for the Block Parent Program to be introduced in "every city, town, and hamlet in this country" and justified the movement in terms of the safety of children, women's traditional role as protector of children, and a greater role of advocacy for women in their community. Margaret MacGee, who was not part of the NCJW but was instrumental in assisting new communities who wished to adopt Block Parent, became an adviser on the central committee for the program. MacGee remarked that Block Parent was "a natural program for housewives and mothers, and fathers who are home in the evening ... It is especially suited to the mother who is at home with either preschool children or very small children because she is at home more than the mother of older children" (Morris, 1976, p. 8). Appealing to the importance of the program, the "natural" role of young mothers, fears about child safety, and the ease of the mechanics of starting one up, Morris stated, "if you're ever worried about your children's safety in the current climate of increasing violence, read on" (Morris, 1976, p. 7).

"Where It Once Took a Village, It Now Takes a Device": The Rise and Fall of the Block Parent Program

With the advocacy of the National Council of Jewish Women, Eileen Morris's call to the readership of *Homemakers* to have a Block Parent home in every city, town, and hamlet across Canada was becoming a reality. By the fall of 1970, the newly established Block Parent Program protected all but one of London's school areas (Block Parent Program of Canada, 1990, p. 3). The original members of the Public Affairs Committee of NCJW were involved in the program for about four years until London City Council took the Block Parent Program under its wing in 1972, forming the Block Parents Central Committee, a subcommittee of the City of London Safety subcommittee. During this time, police reported a decline in overall crime in London, suggesting that the Block Parent signs were acting as deterrents. Moreover, police noted a decrease in offences against children in London and an associated increase in child-related crimes in London's outlying areas.

Consequently, over the next decade, Block Parent spread to many smaller communities outside of London including Hamilton (1969), Sarnia (1971), St. Thomas (1972), and the Region of Waterloo (1977).[1] Shortly afterwards, the program spread across the country. The first program established outside of Ontario was in Edmonton, Alberta, in 1973, and from there programs were established in both mid-sized towns and major Canadian cities in Manitoba (1975), Quebec, and British Columbia (1976).[2]

In the 1970s, Block Parent slowly gained popularity and momentum, attracting sponsors and partnerships that began to accelerate its growth. The Canada Safety Council promoted the program widely[3] and a number of high-profile individuals became interested in involvement with the Block Parent Program. At this time, executive boards were formed, media outlets enthusiastically marketed the program, and corporate sponsorship was readily available.

The program was seen to be a panacea to address a broad spectrum of social problems. In addition to providing help to a child that might be injured, bullied, lost, or scared by a dog, in 1979, the Block Parent model was being studied by the Peel Intercommunity Relations Association, which was set up to address serious offences including racially motivated attacks. James Harding from Peel Regional Police, a founding member of the anti-racism association, said that a Block Parent approach would reassure a young victim of racial attacks or taunts that there was somewhere to turn. Robin Sarkar, the association chairman, said that Block Parent neighbourhoods would facilitate the spread of racial harmony.[4] Moreover, it was thought that with the right training, a skilled Block Parent could even address serious cases of family incest. Dr. George Phills, a psychologist with the London Board of Education, instructed Block Parent volunteers at a training workshop not to appear shocked if a young person disclosed molestation within the family, specifically because the Block Parent may know the parent or guardian of that child.[5] While the inception of Block Parent revolved around stranger danger, it was seen as relevant to some of the actual risks facing children and youth, such as child abuse. However, there was also inordinate faith given to the Block Parent to address serious (domestic and racially motivated) matters.

In communities across Canada, the Block Parent Program boasted a positive reputation and was viewed as a viable solution when a community was faced with a crime or tragedy related to a child (see figure 4 showing children marketing the program to potential adult volunteers). For example, in the City of Winnipeg, after a child molestation took place in 1975, community meetings were held to address child safety and the result was that the Block Parent Program was adopted in response to this tragedy.[6] There continued to be a strong belief in the ability of the program to protect youth using a routine activities approach. Ten years after the start of the Block Parent Program, there were 250 Block Parent communities in Canada and the Canada Safety Council continued to support the program's growth, holding national meetings of its membership and honouring volunteers such as Margaret MacGee, who was so influential in building the program.[7]

The rapid growth continued into the 1980s. Block Parent continued to gain popularity and attract high-profile involvement. In 1981 the governor general's wife, Lily Schreyer, became a Block Parent and flew the Block Parent flag over Rideau Hall. Only two years later, in 1983, Mme Jeanne Sauvé, governor general of Canada, became the patron of the National Block Parent Program (BC Crime Prevention Association, 1988). Even Canadian singer songwriter Ian Thomas and his wife

Figure 4. Children Marketing the Block Parent Program in 1974. Block Parents
Need Help – Joey Connolly, 4, left, and his brother Michael, 7, 106 Elm Street,
hold a sign asking all interested adults to volunteer to be Block Parents. The
Block Parents organization needs help in some areas of the city.
Source: Elgin County Archives, *St. Thomas Times Journal*, 8 October 1974.

Catherine were Block Parents.[8] The program continued to gain momentum, mostly in rural towns and smaller communities, and included both
small businesses and some large-scale businesses that endorsed and
supported the program (see figure 5 for small businesses like Schreit-
er's Furniture store promoting the Block Parent Program). For instance,
the "Inco Triangle," a company newsletter for employees of Inco Metals
Company in Sudbury, Ontario, highlighted the newly formed Sudbury
Block Parent Association in 1981. Bill Thompson, chairman of the Sudbury Jaycees organizing committee for the program noted that of the
3,000 Block Parents in Sudbury, one-third were Inco employees. As
cautioned by Thompson, "there isn't an area in this region that isn't
immune to a child being molested or physically abused." Employees of
Inco were doing their part (Inco Metals Company, 1981, p. 14).

Figure 5. Small Business Promoting the Block Parent Program in 1976.
Credit: @WatBlockParents via X, 2 June 2022. T. Mondou

In the Ontario Legislative Assembly in 1982, MP W. Donald Cousens made a case for "watch" programs including Block Parent referring to the need to go back to a time of neighbourly concern as could be seen in smaller towns and communities. He noted that the official systems (police, courts, and corrections) were diligent in their work but that these institutions of justice had their limits and needed expansion through neighbourhood networks. As stated by MP Cousens:

> we need something more, something that existed among the early pioneers of Canada as they took an interest in one another and each kept an eye out for their neighbours. There was, years ago, a spirit of neighbourliness and concern for those around them that has been lost to some degree in today's society.
>
> Some of that old-fashioned interest in one's neighbour is coming back today because of the increase in crime. ...A policeman patrolling might not recognize a stranger in one's yard but a neighbour would.[9]

The appeal to a lost sense of community from years past is a theme that is pervasive in relation to Block Parent, and this kind of sentiment added fuel to the program's drive towards a more formal, national organization. This momentum continued into the early 1980s when a National Block Parent Committee was formed, the Block Parent Program of Canada was incorporated,[10] and the first National Block Parent Program meeting was held in Ottawa on 17 October 1983 with representatives from all provinces and territories in attendance (BPOC Official Motions, 1983). According to the Annual Reports, one of the principal challenges of the Block Parent Program of Canada was the maintenance of a uniform high standard within the program throughout the vast network of volunteers by setting guidelines to which member communities needed to operate. To this end, the National Board guaranteed the credibility of the program (Block Parent Program of Canada, 1991, p. 2).

Indeed, the integrity of the program was of utmost importance, as was the other side of the coin – concerns about the liability of ordinary citizens as interveners in a potential conflict and so-called safe strangers. Early in the program, the advice given to volunteers was that they "should do nothing that common sense wouldn't dictate," according to Charmaine Haddad of the North York Block Parents Association. However, as Haddad explained, like any other citizen who steps in and tries to help "another in peril, the block parent is exposed to civil liability if the assistance is bungled."[11] With appropriate training and oversight, Block Parents would understand their duties, use common sense, and would be accountable to the program through the completion of incident reports and knowing when to call the police (see figure 6). The program had abundant sponsorship to produce training materials for volunteers, in addition to public promotion through schools, bilingual brochures, posters, newspapers, radio announcements, real estate branch counter signs, annual conference programs, and materials for committee use such as name badges.

In 1987, the copyright for the Block Parent trademark and symbol was transferred from the Canada Safety Council to the National Program, Block Parent of Canada. The program's success enabled "Block Parent Weeks" to be held by different organizations such as the Calgary Block Parent Association, which held a fundraising ceremony for 12,000 Block Parent volunteers in 1989. By the 1990s, the program had over 500,000 households in over 1,000 communities (Block Parent Program of Canada, 1990, p. 6–7); only five years later, in 1995, the number of households was reduced by almost half, with approximately 247,000 participating homes in 1,039 communities across Canada (Block Parent Program of Canada, 1995, p. 5).[12] Even still, the overall membership

Figure 6. Block Parents Do Not Interfere if They See a Crime in Progress, but They Do Call the Police.
Source: British Columbia Crime Prevention Association, 1988.

was still robust as noted in the 1996 Block Parent Annual Report, which indicated there were over 500,000 active Block Parent members from coast to coast (Block Parent Program of Canada, 1996, p. 5).

Latchkey Kids

One of the reasons that membership numbers were declining was because the model upon which Block Parent was premised – volunteers comprised of stay-at-home women – was dramatically shifting. In the 1960s and early 1970s, the program was easier to operate because, as noted by Margaret MacGee, it was a natural extension to the work already being provided by housewives and mothers (Morris, 1976). However, this changed in the following decades as women entered the workforce in substantial numbers. In 1968, 37.5 per cent of women between the ages of 25–54 worked outside of the home. Ten years later, more than half (56.2 per cent) of women in this age group worked outside of the home, and by 1988, two-thirds (73.1 per cent) of women worked outside the home (Milan, 2015). With women working outside of the home, another concern about child safety ironically emerged – worries about "latchkey" children, so named because they wore a house key around their necks to gain entry to their empty home after school and spent large portions of their time unsupervised until a parent returned after the workday. The consequences of women in the workforce leaving unsupervised children were significant. As pointed out in a 1982 report from the Edmonton Committee on the Preservation of Out of School Care, in Edmonton alone there were 32,000 to 40,000 latchkey kids between the ages of five and fourteen with mothers that worked outside of the home, and 10 per cent were from single-parent families. Latchkey kids were thought to be suffering from anxiety, frustration, and alienation; they were more likely to run away from home, play hooky, engage in drug abuse, and delinquency; and they were more at risk for suicide.[13] Research on latchkey children during this period of time did not support these conclusions. Few differences were noted between supervised and unsupervised children in terms of school achievement, social adjustment, attitudes, and personal development (Taveggia & Thomas, 1974). Furthermore, unsupervised children were not more delinquent, accident-prone, or in need of psychological referrals than supervised children (Fosarelli, 1984, p. 175).

Regardless, the concerns about latchkey kids led to the need for solutions such as after-school programs, especially in large urban areas. According to Betty Hodge, manager of the St. Thomas-Elgin Information Centre, "in small towns such as Port Stanley, Ontario, after-school childcare still means a trip to Grandma's, the neighbour's or the babysitter's. People make their own arrangements." However, the concerns were quite different in larger cities. Elizabeth Fawcett from the Toronto YMCA stated that having "kids on the loose" is not too much trouble in smaller towns but "in cities such as Toronto and North York, the time has long passed when working parents could rely on a neighbourly hand to supervise their school- age children. It's totally impractical to assume there's a friendly neighbour nearby when advising kids on how to stay home alone." To that end, the guide produced by the YWCA called "Latchkey Kids" recommended that parents should make arrangements for a "designated" adult to go to in case of an emergency. According to Ms. Fawcett, "that person may have to be a local shopkeeper or, in an apartment, the building supervisor, if there are no neighbors available." To address this issue, Toronto established a "warm line" in 1983, which was a phone-in counselling service set up for children who were home alone. This "innovative service" received between 70 and 250 calls a day and was financed by the Ministry of Community and Social Services.[14]

The diminishing guardianship of Block Parent was having an impact on children in many ways – with more women in the workforce, more children were left unsupervised and no longer could kids rely on a friendly neighbour or the availability of a Block Parent home.

Putting the Community Back in the Fight against Crime

Despite their declining numbers, the Block Parent Program continued to have high-profile involvement in the 1990s such as sustained and strong support from the governor general of Canada, robust police support and community partnerships, and the opening of a national office near Toronto, Ontario. The movement towards the responsibilization of communities to work alongside law enforcement authorities – as partners – in order to prevent and control crime was central to this shift (O'Malley & Palmer, 1996; Garland, 2001; Johnston & Shearing, 2002).

In Vancouver, there were 16,000 registered Block Parent households and a general increase in individuals who were involved or significantly interested in crime prevention.[15] During this time, there was a broadening of networks associated with citizen community programs including Block Watch (similar to Neighbourhood Watch), Block Parents, Citizen Crime Patrols, community police stations, and auxiliary or reserve police officer programs, foreshadowing a merging of different citizen-led programs. While these were all within the scope of community crime prevention broadly speaking, the patrolling of neighbourhoods and more passive "watch" programs were not in keeping with the original ethos of Block Parent. While there is frequently a conflation between different kinds of "watch" programs, Block Parent is distinct. Neighbourhood Watch is about protecting property, whereas Block Parent is about protecting (vulnerable) people.

In the larger context, there was a clear national narrative and an attitude that community-based crime prevention programs worked to prevent crime: specifically, they kept children safe. Although there were no official statistics available to substantiate claims of crime reduction and child safety, the support for, and belief in, the programs' effectiveness was clear and generally endorsed. Moreover, the displacement of potential crime to other, non-Block Parent neighbourhoods fuelled widespread interest in the program. For instance, Constable Bob Copeland, a Metro Toronto police crime prevention officer, noted that "child molesters have told police during questioning that they avoid Block

Parent neighbourhoods," and in terms of overall crime, Copeland further indicated that "when Block Parent programs are set up, the number of break-ins can drop."[16]

Notably though, Simon Fraser University criminologist Paul Brantingham warned that community policing programs by themselves do not work against all types of crime in all areas and that community programs are easiest to set up in middle-class neighbourhoods that do not have serious crime problems. He further elaborated that getting Block Parent or Block Watch programs to catch on in lower-income areas with few long-term residents is more difficult.[17]

Brantingham's concerns are supported by research in this area. For example, Reynald's (2010) study of capable guardianship reported that residents in low crime, higher income, and less ethnically diverse communities were more likely to supervise and intervene (directly or indirectly) in preventing a potential criminal event. The concern is that situational crime prevention approaches such as Block Parent flourish in more socially cohesive, higher income, and generally lower crime areas (Roberts & Hastings, 2007; Reynald, 2010; Mawby, 2019; Varma, 2023). While they may provide a certain perception of safety in these neighbourhoods, it would be important to address the possible need in neighbourhoods that are more at risk of crime and where children are in need of various kinds of protection. As discussed by Roberts & Hastings (2007, p. 214) "voluntary participation tends to be much more problematic in high needs low capacity communities – in other words, the communities that need help the most."

This concern, having Block Parent assistance in the neighbourhoods where help is needed, was articulated a decade later as members of the Special Committee to Prevent the Abuse and Exploitation of Children Through the Sex Trade debated about the best way to deal with this problem. Sergeant Ron Savidan of the La Ronge, Saskatchewan, RCMP detachment stated that the communities that needed Block Parent or watch programs to provide a safe house for children did not have the community "spirit" to organize:

> Our community is made up of about 6,000 people in the town of La Ronge, Air Ronge, the reserve district. We have communities within this community, like areas, neighbourhoods. And the neighbourhoods where we do have Neighbourhood Watch, the drug and alcohol abuse isn't as high as another neighbourhood where it is, and in that neighbourhood we do not have any crime watch or Neighbourhood Watch or Parent because the people that live in that little neighbourhood don't want to be involved with that. They don't have that *community spirit*. So though we have it in

the community, we don't have it in the neighbourhood that it's required in – in the group of homes where there's a lot of drug and alcohol abuse. (Hansard Debates, 2000, p. 342, emphasis added)

While community spirit may have been part of the equation, having time, resources, stability in one's neighbourhood, trust between neighbours, and trust for state institutions such as schools and police were all pertinent for the creation of programs like Block Parent. Nevertheless, the importance of keeping this community "spirit" intact was at the core of much of the work of Block Parent. In addition to recruiting volunteers and setting up new programs, fostering community cohesion was of utmost importance. Annual Reports highlighted the contributions of long-serving members, as well as recognizing volunteers with ceremonies, gold and silver award pins for service, and thank you cards. Community picnics and celebrations were organized to show appreciation for volunteers – even when volunteers indicated that nobody came to their door – to keep the civic engagement, spirit, and mutual trust and fellow feeling in the community thriving (Block Parent Program of Canada; Garland, 2023).

CARE – Children Are the Responsibility of Everyone

Child protection is a generally universal concern. The ideal situation of all neighbourhoods being Block Parent neighbourhoods would address the unevenness noted above so that all children, regardless of neighbourhood, could access safe refuge through neighbourhood homes. Markedly, by the mid-1990s there was a clear framing of child protection being the responsibility of everyone though there was some negative publicity, foreshadowing later concerns, which occurred when Block Parent signs were not removed from the doors of some participating households. During this time, the Block Parent Annual Reports and advertisements promoted the slogan CARE – Children Are the Responsibility of Everyone (see figure 7) (1995 Newsletter, the National Voice of Block Parent).

By 1999, there were pockets of Block Parent and Neighbourhood Watch programs in operation, in some cases working together, some with funding by local police departments. The variation in the program, in many cases triggered by a child abduction or molestation case, resulted in a greater number of Block Parent programs in predominantly middle-class areas, and more often in rural rather than urban areas.[18] One such distressing case occurred on 14 October 1990, when six-year-old Andrea Atkinson disappeared from her apartment

Figure 7. Block Parent Advertisement, 1995.

in the Coxwell and Danforth area of Toronto and was missing for nine days. Tragically, she was found to have been sexually assaulted and murdered in the laundry room of the building where she lived. In February 1993, the caretaker for the building, eighteen-year-old John Terceira, was convicted of her murder. Shortly after Andrea's body was found, the community became home to 1,200 Block Parent households.[19] Once again, the community was grieving and in shock alongside Andrea's family. Something had to be done to protect children, and while Block Parent may not have helped in this case, the community banding together to protect children symbolized the grief and outpouring of anguish at the loss of this child (see figure 8, educating children about the Block Parent Program two weeks after the disappearance of Andrea Atkinson).

There were other kinds of catalysts that ignited resurgence in Block Parent membership, such as when communities were notified of the release of a sex offender, once again directing focus on the danger of strangers. Community notification laws are intended to inform the

Figure 8. Newspaper Article Educating Children about the Block Parent Program, 1990. Block Parents' large red and white sign tells children and others help is available.
Source: Slaughter, M. *Toronto Star/Getty images*, 2 November 1990.

public about the release of a sex offender who may be still considered a threat to public safety despite having completed their sentence. There is an assumption that this knowledge will allow members of the community to take steps to ensure their children's safety and their own, as is the belief in Manitoba.[20] However, a large body of research has noted that the perceived improvements to public safety are not empirically supported and may come at a cost to the public in assuming a false sense of safety through notification and registry measures (Zevitz & Farkas, 2000; Durling, 2006; Bouffard & LaQuana, 2019). Moreover, the effects of public notification can be seen in greater Block Parent involvement but also an expansion of the traditional Block Parent model towards citizen patrols in a widening network of surveillance (Parnaby, 2006; Reeves, 2012). For example, in New Brunswick the release of a convicted sex offender into the Barkers Point neighbourhood sparked crime prevention initiatives in the community.[21] Residents became involved in both the Block Parent and the Neighbourhood Watch programs and patrolled the neighbourhood parks, paths, and schools wearing shirts purchased through fundraising activities and reported suspicious activities to the police. They recounted that as a result of this mobilization, crime in the neighbourhood began to decline, yet these activities (patrolling the neighbourhood) were not based upon the original model nor philosophy of Block Parent.[22]

"We Help Them Feel Safe"

In the latter parts of the 1990s, Block Parent membership was referred to as a "lifestyle attitude" (Block Parent Program of Canada, 1996, 1998). However, there was a marked departure from this approach in the years that followed. As mentioned earlier, in the early decades of the program there was widespread support as it expanded throughout the country, deterred would-be offenders, and created community cohesion around the project of child protection. However, the Annual Reports begin to reveal a shift from the year 2000 onwards. The yearly activities and strategic plans become preoccupied with addressing security concerns that were not present in the prior decades. Post 2000, the Annual Reports demonstrate a clear shift from the promotion of the program to defending the program and highlighting its need. This shift can also be seen in the gradual decline of participating communities and homes. By the start of the '00s, Block Parent membership had dropped to approximately nine hundred communities across Canada (Block Parent Program of Canada, 2000, 2) compared to one thousand communities in 1990 (see figures 9 and 10 showing Block Parent communities, businesses, and homes over a nineteen-year period). Despite its decline over the decades and the changing societal landscape in which the program operated, the Block Parent Program evolved, actively expanding to serve children's needs in other ways (e.g., walking safely to school) and reinforcing its other benefits such as assisting other vulnerable populations in attempts to stay relevant and useful. Initially the program served school-aged children, but its mandate expanded to include teenagers in the 1980s and seniors in the 1990s (Block Parent Program of Canada, 1990, p. 1) and in the late 1990s the program encouraged fire stations and small businesses to become Block Parent locations (Block Parent Program of Canada, 1999, p. 4).

Many prominent events occurred for the Block Parent Program up to the mid-2000s. However, once again, there was variation in the strength of the program, which depended upon the context and location. In Calgary, celebrations for long-serving Block Parents occurred along with renewed interest in the evolution of the program. This included expanding the program to invite small businesses to become involved. As stated by Lynn Squance, executive director of Calgary Block Parent:

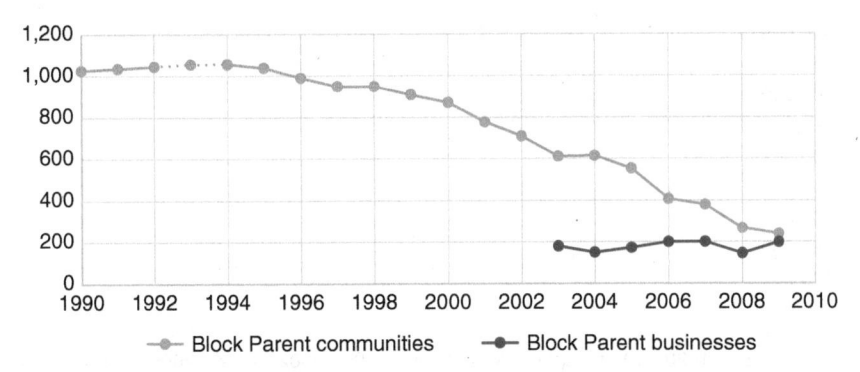

Figure 9. Number of Block Parent Communities and Block Parent Businesses.
Notes: No data for 1993 (estimated in figure 9 as a dotted line). Reporting of statistics on Block Parent communities discontinued in Annual Reports from 2010 onwards. Business Block Parent began reporting in 2003 and discontinued in 2010.
Source: Block Parent Program of Canada Annual Reports (1990–2016).

With fewer parents staying home all day, Block Parent has begun to recruit small businesses as places to post the familiar red and white signs showing a woman holding a child's hand. Corner stores, grocery stores and laundromats are some of the 116 participating ground-floor businesses open during the day with small enough staffs to remain committed.[23]

In 2000, the Guelph, Ontario, Block Parent Program celebrated its twenty-fifth anniversary but was looking to recruit more volunteers.[24] According to media coverage of the time, the program was going strong in rural areas despite the fact that there were not many serious incidents occurring. Block Parent coordinator for Petrolia and district, Ann Selman, discussed the fact that for as long as she could remember, there were no incident reports turned in by Block Parents. "I don't know if anyone uses it … it just lays low."[25] In Ontario, when serious incidents did occur, they were reported to the Ontario Provincial Police. This is noteworthy as the program had strong police involvement in Ontario at the time.[26]

The '00s were a pivotal decade in the trajectory of the program as it began to face difficulties due to decreased funding and a policy change that had significant effects on the sparse remaining volunteer workforce. The new policy dictated that volunteers, not just those over eighteen but anyone over the age of twelve, would need to be rescreened every two years, and unless the local police force was still participating in the program, the fee would have to now be paid by the

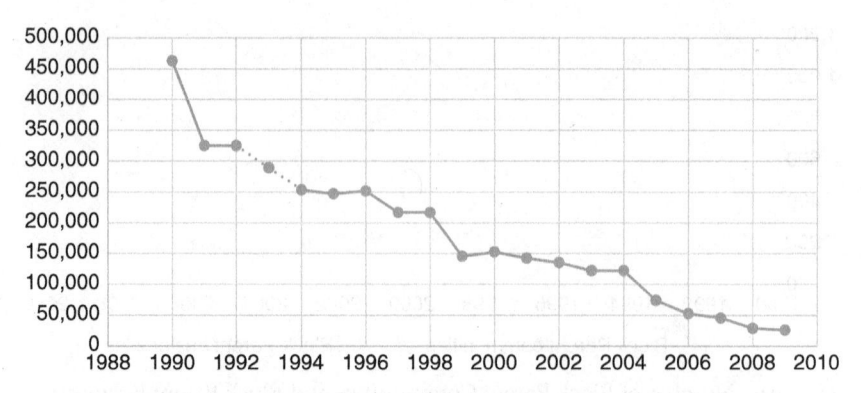

Figure 10. Number of Block Parents Homes in Canada, Annual Reports.
Note: No data for 1993 (estimated in figure 10 as a dotted line). Reporting of statistics on Block Parent homes discontinued in Annual Reports from 2010 onwards.
Source: Block Parent Program of Canada Annual Reports (1990–2016).

volunteer(s). This policy change meant that "every person in the Block Parent household over twelve years old would have to be screened and this would have cost a large amount of money."[27] Additionally, the competition for funding changed significantly because the model of Block Parent did not fit with other crime prevention programs. In reflecting on the way funding occurred in the early stages versus later, one of the interviewees noted the challenges:

> Block Parents did not fit any type of mould because we are not an in-your-face program; we are a very quiet program. When we first started getting funding from the feds [federal government], we were in with people like John Howard and Elizabeth Fry. We are not like them and we did not fit the mould, but that is where they put us. But then it went to thirteen organizations that all got funding and we really didn't have to do much – we just had to send them an Annual Report. And that was really all we had to do and let them know what our numbers were and the Annual Report, and they sent us a cheque ... and it was just in the last eight years, nine years that changed and we lost our funding.

Around the same time that other Block Parent communities were facing financial cutbacks, as a result of the initiative of particular volunteers' networking abilities and creativity, Winnipeg Block Parent was able to utilize a yearly operating grant from the City of Winnipeg towards the hiring of part-time staff and renovating an office for Block Parent use

Figure 11. Trusty the Bear at a Block Parent Function in Winnipeg.
Photo credit: George Jarvis.

in a city-owned building. The Winnipeg Block Parent Program in the mid-2000s was running strong and was focused on building a robust program by taking on initiatives using new technology such as Google Earth mapping[28] in order to showcase the number of membership homes and to help people to know where to find help. At this time, the first social media platforms for Block Parent, such as Facebook groups, began to emerge as well. In addition, a promotional mascot named "Trusty the Bear" was created to educate elementary school children about the program.[29]

Despite this momentum, Winnipeg also experienced a drop in membership numbers from previous years. Membership was down by six hundred homes and it took five years to confirm this decline in membership status due to difficulties in contacting volunteers. However, despite the larger policy shifts that occurred in the year 2000 that impacted the operation of the program nationally, the city and police in Winnipeg continued to support the Block Parent Program. The national policy shift of requiring police checks for membership impacted

Winnipeg less negatively because police checks in Winnipeg were set up to be completed online at no cost with the support and continued cooperation of the police department. Another check, the required child abuse registry check, was completed through the provincial registry of Child and Family Services through the mail, also at no cost. There were other crime prevention programs running in Winnipeg, such as Neighbourhood Watch and Community Citizens on Patrol, which were administered by the police. Winnipeg was unique in having a roster of community crime prevention programs working in tandem, such as Bear Clan and Mama Bear Clan Patrols,[30] which were formed during this time. Both of these Bear Clan programs are community advocacy groups, the latter of which is focused on safety, healing, and matriarchal leadership of Indigenous women and was created by the North Point Douglas Women's Warrior Circle.

Background Checks, Accountability, and Integrity of the Block Parent Signs

By 2001, police checks were required for every member in a Block Parent household over twelve years of age (Block Parent Program of Canada, 2000), which aimed at enhanced scrutiny and security. This can be understood within broader changes in society and in the criminal justice system towards the governance of individualized risks and accountability (O'Malley, 2006; Garland, 2001).

Coincidentally, in March of 2001, a high-ranking volunteer with the New Brunswick Block Parent Association was charged with fraud over $5,000 after an investigation by the Saint John Police Force. The fraudulent offences occurred between January 1997 and September 2000 and involved a Block Parent treasurer of the local program. This individual pleaded guilty to stealing more than $38,000 from the association and was sentenced to house arrest for a period of two years.[31] While this was widely reported in the media, the Block Parent Program did not suffer reputational damage, and it appears to be the only time that something of this nature occurred. Two months after these occurrences, the National Block Parent Convention was held in New Brunswick in April and events were carried out routinely.

In the following years, programs across the country experienced an array of different successes and challenges. For example, anti-crime activities were being funded in the Yukon from the federal government's National Strategy on Community Safety. Among the many projects being funded out of a total of $1.3 million in federal spending, Crime Prevention Yukon received $8,300 for the Block Parent Program in 2002.[32]

In Ontario, five existing Block Parent programs in the Greater Toronto Area formed a single group, though organizers of the Scarborough program decided to remain independent because their program was thriving.[33] In Sault Saint Marie, a Block Parent float was celebrated in the community day parade.[34]

However, by 2003 the widespread decline of the program's operations, popularity, support, and sponsorship can be clearly mapped. During this time, various police agencies began to rescind their support for the program. Between 2002 and 2006 the Royal Canadian Mounted Police (RCMP), the Toronto Police Service, and York Regional Police withdrew their support for the Block Parent Program amid liability concerns.[35] As cautioned by Sergeant Rod Radborn of the Toronto Police: "We're saying these are safe havens and if you don't believe in your own mind that they're safe, you shouldn't be advising the public they are ... The program requires a change or it will go by the wayside. It's a sad thing, but I had such serious concerns that from a risk-management perspective, I could no longer support it."[36] Three years later, similar concerns were raised by York Regional Police Constable Laurie Perks, in this case, warning about stranger danger, but this time in the form of Block Parent *volunteers*. "In this day and age, there are other alternatives to having a child go to a home of a person they don't know ... even with the background checks, do we really want to take that kind of risk?"[37] The concept of Block Parents considered to be "safe strangers" as referred to in early Block Parent materials was no longer viable and added to the police and public's mistrust of the program.

The lack of police support for the program had a significant impact because it meant that required background checks could no longer be completed free of charge for residents in these areas, and vitally it also signalled that the police no longer believed in the program. Given the close partnerships with the police during the inception and growth of the program, this was a dramatic shift. The 2003 Block Parent Annual Report noted that the year had proven to be a challenge, in large part due to the Toronto Police Force withdrawing its support "without any prior warning" and also due to staffing issues in the Barrie head office (Block Parent Program of Canada, 2003, p. 1). Concerns about liability had an enormous impact on the program. As part of the screening process, Block Parent administrators were required to carry out home visits for prospective volunteers. As noted by one interviewee:

> We have ten steps to screening, so now you have to have a house visit even before you get your sign because at the time we were with an insurance company. We had to make sure that getting to the door there were no

obstacles, or pets, no dogs that was [sic] going to scare the children going into the home, to make sure you had a good feeling when you went into the home. We had references, we started asking for references.

The challenges facing Block Parent were many: a lack of funding, increasing hurdles for would-be volunteers – screening, home visits, paying for police checks – as well as a police mistrust of screened volunteers, all in a climate where family structure had changed and people had limited time.

Despite the challenges, program sponsorship continued and there was progress on an initiative started by the Block Parent organization to create a national database called BPLINK, which facilitated the entering of data in Block Parent programs across the country and added to the accountability of the program. Additionally, volunteers continued to work tirelessly, providing a total of 986 million hours across Canada in 2003. These volunteers, along with approximately two hundred Business Block Parent locations, allowed the program to continue to survive (Block Parent Program of Canada, 2003).

While volunteers kept the program alive, through the next several years, sponsorship slowly declined, and the program lost popularity. Crucially, it began to lose funding for its activities. As illustrated in figure 11, sponsorship from 1990 onwards was strong and consistent, but after 2008, it fell to two sponsors – the Co-operators and Public Safety/Solicitor General Canada.

Public Safety was a consistent sponsor throughout. In 2002 and 2003, First Pro Shopping Centres (later Smart Centres) donated considerable funds to the program with an expectation of ongoing funding. However, due to the Toronto Police withdrawal of support, First Pro/Smart Centres "reconsidered" their funding but decided to continue. However, Cadbury Beverages, a brand-new sponsor, decided to withdraw its financial support for the program due to the Toronto Police situation (Block Parent Program of Canada, 2003). See figure 12 showing National Sponsors for the Block Parent Program.

In 2003, the National Block Parent Program announced that in order to be a designated Block Parent household, all households would now have to be contacted yearly in addition to the criminal record check of all household residents over the age of twelve.[38] Yearly background checks had to be coordinated on the BPLINK database, adding to the privacy concerns of volunteers. The mandate that everyone in a household above the age of twelve had to be checked for a criminal record was proving to be increasingly complex and problematic. It prevented many families from signing up and remaining as Block Parents due to

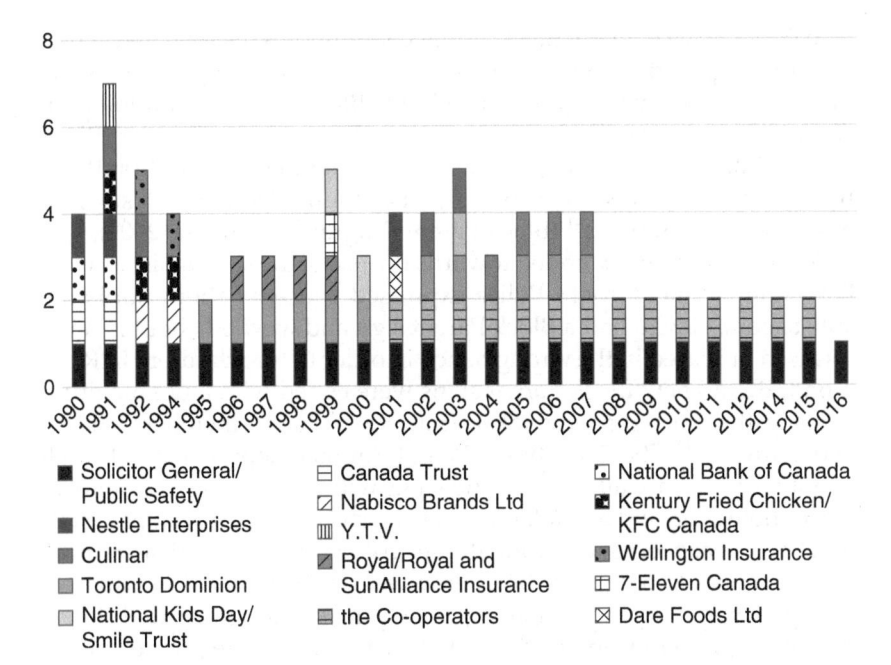

Figure 12. National Sponsors for Block Parent Program of Canada Annual Reports (1990–2016).
Notes: Annual Reports for the years 1993 and 2013 were not available.
Source: Block Parent Program of Canada Annual Reports (1990–2016).

personal concerns, such as past histories or reports of alcohol problems, previous contact with the criminal justice or youth justice system, and even owning aggressive pets.[39]

Particular communities, such as British Columbia's Prince Rupert and Port Edward, went even further in terms of security. It was announced that as of 30 January 2003 entire families would have to be fingerprinted in addition to undergoing a criminal record check if they wanted to display the Block Parent sign in their window.[40] The closure of other programs, including the Richmond Block Parent Program, occurred after decisions were made by the BC Block Party Society and RCMP detachments due to the lack of parent volunteer support. Executives of the program acknowledged that the initial model of the Block Parent Program was not viable anymore since there were few "stay-at-home moms" and the lack of volunteers proved to be a serious problem for many communities.

In the same year, many Block Parent communities disappeared across Ontario, in part due to the increased scrutiny given to volunteers. By March 2003, there were approximately 145 Block Parent communities in Ontario, half the number of communities about a decade earlier (Block Parent Program of Canada, 1995). Active programs were in Brantford, Burford, Paris, St. George, Scotland, and Mount Pleasant – all small to mid-sized communities[41] (Block Parent Program of Canada, 2003).

Security concerns extended towards the use of the sign again, as well. For example, the Toronto Police expressed concerns about not being able to control who had a Block Parent sign and worried about it being misused or placed in the wrong hands in order to lure children. In Richmond, BC, all new Block Parent signs were coded with a unique number, and the old signs were taken from Block Parent members, coded, and returned.[42] The 2003 Block Parent Annual Report instructed all members to replace all pictures and signs with the more secure version, with a hologram and a validation sticker that had been developed, stating, "due to concerns regarding the security of the logo and sign, more secure images of both have been provided on the national website." A new policy and position paper regarding the signs was drafted (Block Parent Program of Canada, 2003, p. 2). Three years later, there was an effort to work with policing partners across Canada to address various safety concerns and to develop a new Block Parent window sign with changed security features. Subsequently, each community was asked to conduct risk assessments (Block Parent Program of Canada 2006, p. 2).

While the number of Block Parent communities was declining amid concerns about nefarious intent with the use of signs and the security of a Block Parent home, terrible events once again brought forward calls to bring back the program. Following the tragic kidnapping and murder of ten-year-old Holly Jones in Toronto in May of 2003, Block Parents wondered how they could make their program relevant again in large urban communities where child safety concerns were not being adequately addressed. Only five months after Holly Jones went missing, nine-year-old Cecilia Zhang was abducted from her North York bedroom. Tragically, her body was found in March 2004. After these devastating incidents, communities were in shock, once again raising concerns about the closing of Block Parent programs and the gap that was left in terms of child safety given the two missing children within months of each other in the Greater Toronto Area.[43] In smaller communities across the country, there was a renewed energy to invigorate and expand the program. In New Brunswick, there were celebrations for long-serving Block Parent members who were honoured with Queen's Golden Jubilee Medals.[44] In Fredericton, 150 new Block Parent homes were reported in the media, reinforcing the original view that the Block Parent sign means safety. The uneven distribution of Block Parent programs continued – while membership dropped and the program closed down in some communities, successful pockets of the program could be found across the country. For example, the program thrived in Kawartha Lakes but ultimately closed its doors in November of 2006 due to a lack of volunteers and increased security.[45]

In the mid-2000s, it was evident that the success of the program depended on the number of invested volunteers in specific communities' and the partnerships and support they were able to secure. In 2005, there were reports of many Block Parent communities closing doors, and the BC Block Parent Society asked volunteers to remove their signs from homes.[46] In the following years, program membership continued to decline with approximately one hundred Block Parent communities across Ontario in 2006 (Block Parent Program of Canada, 2006).[47] This was the year that York Regional Police formally removed their support for the program, which not only created obstacles for trust in the program, but meant that screening for anyone over the age of twelve who lived in a Block Parent home along with rescreening every two to three years was no longer free. When the York Block Parent Program closed, support was removed from every community in the Greater Toronto Area where there was no longer police support, with the exception of Durham Region, where screenings remained free.[48] The discussion surrounding police support became increasingly preoccupied with safety concerns, liability, and an overall lack of belief in the program. Marg Rooke, chairperson of the Ontario Block Parents Program, saw this as the end, remarking, "with a lack of police support we simply cannot function." However, Rooke questioned the notion of risk put forward by the police, maintaining that the Block Parent had a track record of safety for young people and stories about people with intentions of harming children posing as Block Parents to try to lure them into their homes were "simply fictional." She further indicated that these were rumors, and nothing had ever been substantiated nor was there any documentation of a single incident in which a child was ever harmed at a Block Parent home.

There were other rumours that circulated about the Block Parent Program that raised some concerns but were purely speculative. Nevertheless, apprehension about the program prevailed. The other challenge that continued to persist, apart from innuendo about child luring and misuse of signs, was the lack of volunteers. As explained by Anna Greig, a long-time Markham Block Parent and chairperson of the local arm of the organization, which closed in 2005, the lack of volunteers, absence of civic engagement, concerns about trust, and worries about liability were a large part of the problem:

> People know less about their neighbours, care less about their communi-
> ties, and are even more concerned about liability. These days, people are
> afraid to volunteer. They're afraid to get involved and be put in a position
> where a little kid can say something about them. It's about looking after
> your own, and that's it.[49]

RCMP and Risk Assessment

By 2007, the decline was profound. There were roughly 45,000 Block Parent homes in 379 communities compared to 500,000 Block Parents in 1,000 communities in 1990 (Block Parent Program of Canada, 1990, 1997). Most notably, in late 2006, the RCMP commissioned a risk assessment on the Block Parent Program that resulted in further policy changes that required all Block Parent window signs to be collected and reissued with a serial number (though the Block Parent Program was already working on many of the policy recommendations noted by the RCMP). Window signs were retrieved and new signs with serial numbers were distributed (Block Parent Program of Canada, 2007, p. 2).

The RCMP Block Parent Risk Assessment was national in scope with voluntary participation and was conducted from August to October, 2006. According to the report, overall, the governance framework established by the Block Parent Program of Canada, Inc. was considered appropriate for the mission and mandate of the program. The framework reflected a close working relationship and a de facto partnership between the Block Parent Program and its policing partners and recognized this relationship as central to its continued success (Lansdowne Technologies, 2006, p. i). The impetus for the report was to identify the threats to the program, identify and evaluate the current safeguards and protective measures in place to safeguard Block Parent assets, determine risk associated with the program, and provide recommendations (Lansdowne Technologies, 2006, p. ii). The risk assessment was based on research of available documentation provided by the RCMP and the Block Parent Program as well as direct input provided by over thirty Block Parent stakeholders through formal phone interviews and survey questionnaires. The assessment concluded that the Block Parent bylaws and policies were reasonable and based on sound practices; however, select local programs were said to be experiencing difficulties in meeting program requirements. Further acknowledging that the success of a program was not geographically dependent, in that successes and challenges were noted in both urban and rural programs, the report noted that local program successes could be attributed to a dedicated core group of volunteers or paid employees and a professional and supportive relationship with local law enforcement. Overall, the threat to the Block Parent Program as well as to the RCMP and its law enforcement partners was assessed as "low" and the overall risk assumed by the RCMP and its law enforcement partners was determined to be "medium-low."[50]

The RCMP report provided several key recommendations intended to mitigate the risks associated with day-to-day Block Parent Program operations that included developing a risk-management strategy, determining best practices to attract and recruit new volunteers, conducting risk assessments every three to five years and conducting regular evaluations and audits on the program, creating BPLINK for the management of operations (though this was already in motion years before the RCMP assessment), and safeguarding window signs including the retrieval of old signs and the assignment of serial numbers to new signs (Lansdowne Technologies, 2006).

Finding volunteers and the resources to retrieve all of the old window signs in order to have them replaced with new signs and serial numbers was a monumental task. This, along with the requirement of entering volunteers in the database, created enormous obstacles for an already declining program.

Despite the overall decline, and as indicated in the RCMP risk assessment report, certain locations were more successful than others due, in large part, to a dedicated core group of volunteers. Winnipeg, Manitoba, was one such location. In Winnipeg, new signs were introduced with updated signage that included a provincial sticker and a marker indicating when the sign was issued. This allowed the Winnipeg police services, which remained supportive of the program, to keep track of the signs. Winnipeg Block Parent was unique in sustaining police support, even offering tips to trick-or-treaters and their parents for Halloween: "If you are in need of assistance, go to a Block Parent home."[51]

In stark contrast, the Block Parent Program was discontinued in Ottawa in 2009 since nobody was willing to manage the program. The seventy-nine remaining Ottawa Block Parents were asked to turn in their signs even though the national Block Parent organization had initiated a renewal of the program with increased safety measures and greater accountability only two years earlier.[52]

Despite national general meetings including a celebration of the fortieth-year anniversary of Ontario Block Parent (Block Parent Program of Canada, 2008, p. 2) and Block Parent marketing campaigns boasting

Figure 13. Offices of the Block Parent Program of Winnipeg.
Photo credit: George Jarvis.

over forty years of the program and renewed interest from volunteers (Block Parent Program of Canada, 2009, p. 2), the integrity of the signs, a lack of belief and support for the program from police, and an absence of new volunteers was evident. A steep decline in the membership was also experienced when all old window signs were recalled, and new signs were required to be registered on the BPLINK database between 2008 to 2009, based on the RCMP recommendations. The technological changes resulted in the loss of many Block Parent households, particularly excluding those with limited computer and internet access. As discussed by one of the administrators of the program, this was the final straw:

> When we finalized the new window signs, we called in all the old window signs and coordinators. They had to be on BPLINK – that would have been around 2008, 2009 when that happened. From 1968 to 2000 you could run the program from your kitchen table, but now you couldn't anymore because we wanted you to be in the database, and that's when people said I don't have a computer, or I don't know how to use a computer, or we can't

get Wi-Fi where we live ... That's when we lost the majority of the signs and communities. That was the year we took the big hit.

In 2009, the ebbs and flows of the program continued. There were reports of Block Parent vanishing from homes across the country, and at the same time the resurrection of the program in communities such as Durham, Waterloo, and Fort Erie, Ontario. As noted in the 2009 Annual Report, almost 29,000 Block Parents contributed to twenty-one million volunteer hours and half a million hours were contributed by 144 Block Parent business locations (Block Parent Program of Canada, 2009, p. 4).

Safe Arrival and Amber Alerts

Within an overall climate of declining interest in Block Parent, concerns about child safety came back to the forefront after the tragic abduction and murder of Tori Stafford in Woodstock, Ontario. Eight-year-old Tori was lured away by Terri-Lynn McClintic and Michael Rafferty as she was leaving, unaccompanied, to walk home from Oliver Stephens Public School on 8 April 2009. There was community outrage that the police did not issue an "Amber Alert," named after Amber Hagerman, a nine-year-old child who was abducted while riding her bike in Texas in 1996. After Tori went missing, there was enormous frustration that the police had such strict guidelines for issuing an Amber Alert as people felt that a child missing should be the only criterion. Linda Patterson, Block Parent president, who played a role in introducing the Amber Alert system in New Brunswick, said the reason for sticking to the rigid criteria is to ensure the public doesn't become desensitized.[53]

The tragedy that occurred in the Tori Stafford case reinforced the fundamental purpose of Block Parent: the safety of children as they made their way to and from school and fears of stranger abduction as had occurred back in 1968 with Frankie Jensen. Jensen's parents were not notified until the end of the school day that he had not made it to school, critically delaying the search for the young boy (Arntfield, 2015). In 1968, the Public Affairs Committee of the NCJW noted that school notification was of paramount importance and incorporated this idea into the original Block Parent model. If there was not a secretary to inform the parents, then Block Parent volunteers could take on this kind of role. As noted in the call to action of *Homemakers* magazine:

While the children are learning protective lessons from the police, they are being guarded by another procedure instigated by the Block Parent program. At the start of the school year, principals send home a notice requesting that parents assist the school by sending a note with another child when one child is to be absent, or by telephoning the school before 9:30 a.m. – preferably the note, to keep phones clear (Morris, 1976, p. 12).

The coordination between school and home was significant, and if completed in a systematic way, it would greatly minimize the chances that a child could go missing. Moreover, security over who could pick up a child was crucial. As stated by Constable Huizinga in 1976 *Homemakers*, "if a person claims to be a relative – I'm his uncle – there's *no way* our schools will permit that person to take a child away" (Morris, 1976, p. 14, emphasis in original).

Still Here, Still Helping, Still Needed ...

While broadcast communications such as Amber Alerts and Safe Arrival systems could protect children to a certain extent, the home as safe haven approach of Block Parent was still under scrutiny, mostly focused on who might "get their hands on" the sign, which exacerbated waning support from police and a lack of cooperation from schools.[54]

In 2009, the British Columbia Block Parent Program closed after concerns were raised that Block Parent signs could be copied by people with ill intent. Block Parent president, Linda Patterson, lamented about the program closure in the province of British Columbia and summed up many of the factors that led to the programs' decline:

> We lost a whole province. That had a huge impact. We have tried every single thing under the sun to get that province back ... Studies have shown the program poses no risks ... All volunteers are regularly screened by police. But the new restrictions on signs and the increased requirements for police screening have actually contributed to the program's decline. People who have been Block Parents for twenty or thirty years have decided it wasn't worth the bother to continue to volunteer. They just turned in their signs and didn't get replacements.
>
> When the program was first introduced in Canadian schools, children ran home begging their mothers, and less often their fathers, to participate. It was a status symbol to belong to a Block Parent family. That changed as fewer and fewer moms stayed home to take care of their own kids, which meant they weren't home to rescue the children belonging to neighbours. There are more mothers at work. There are more single parent families in which the parent has to work. That's why our numbers have been going down ... In fact a person does not need to be a stay-at-home parent to be a Block Parent. To be a Block Parent does not mean you need to have that

sign in the window 24/7 ... An hour a day, a half hour a day, might be the most important time that somebody walks by and needs your help.[55]

A year later, in 2010, the National Block Parent Week theme was "Still Here, Still Helping, Still Needed" (Block Parent Program of Canada, 2010, p. 2). The challenges for the program were discussed in the president's message, noting that the new screening requirements put in place by the RCMP were causing longer wait times and that Block Parents were having to be fingerprinted after their applications were submitted (Block Parent Program of Canada, 2010). Nevertheless, strategic planning, marketing, and recruiting of volunteers continued along with sponsorship for the program and recognition of volunteers (Block Parent Program of Canada, 2010).

"Where Once It Took a Village, It Now Takes a Device"

In the following years, the original Block Parent Program in London, Ontario, held a Family Fun Golf fundraiser in an attempt to expand its reach into neighbourhoods with the existing Business Block Parent Program and "Block Walk" Program. Both London and Waterloo, Ontario, introduced "Block Walk," which provided Block Parent approved volunteers who established a "walking school bus" route for added safety, security, and help while children were travelling to and from school (see figure 14, Waterloo Regional Block Parent Walking School Bus Pilot).[56]

However, despite attempts to revive, adapt, and evolve the program, in addition to the security concerns and the significant decline in volunteers, a fundamental shift in the supervision of children continued the declining course of the Block Parent Program. One major technological change was the use of cell phones and other GPS tracking devices while young people were away from their homes, making the Block Parent model less relevant. However, individuals that have been involved in the administration of the Block Parent Program still see the value of having an immediate response. One interviewee remarked on how society has changed such that protection is now offered by cell phones:

Parents say, "he has a cell phone, he doesn't need a Block Parent home," and I say well by the time he pulls the phone out, dials 911, gets someone on the phone, asks for help, they have to send out a police officer, something could happen. Block Parent gave that immediate help. Yes, a cellphone is great, but it can't give you that immediate help that may be needed at that point. Let's say you got someone chasing you, you are running down the street trying to call 911. A lot of parents were saying that my kids got a cellphone, he's fine.

Figure 14. Waterloo Regional Block Parent Program Walking School Bus Pilot Program, St. Anne's Catholic School, Cambridge, 2016.
Credit: T. Mondou, Chair Person, Waterloo Regional Block Parent Program.

The downward trajectory of the Block Parent Program has continued in the last decade. In 2013 there were 25,000 Block Parent homes, mostly in Alberta and Quebec, though programs were shutting down in Ottawa, Toronto, PEI, and much of British Columbia due to a lack of volunteers and concerns regarding the safety of the program. And by 2015, there were 144 Block Parent community programs across Canada administered by a total of three volunteers. These programs consisted of 6,914 homes where one or more police-screened volunteers displayed Block Parent signs.

In 2016 the City of London launched a new competitive process intended to take the politics out of deciding which groups receive grants. As a result, the originators of the program, London Block Parent, closed its doors after losing funding.[57] Most recently, in September of 2018 the Block Parent head office in Barrie, Ontario, closed down as the program no longer had national funding and had lost insurance and support for starting new programs. This meant that the provinces could continue to operate their Block Parent programs, but there would no longer be a centralized national headquarters. As of 2019, there were only nine active Block Parent communities in Ontario.[58]

It is important to mention that despite its fall, the Block Parent Program continues to receive attention and interest from individuals and communities across Canada enquiring about the program and the process to set one up in their community. Overall, the success, engagement, and operations of a given Block Parent Program depended on the volunteers that dedicated their time to it and notably, many volunteers devoted their time and energy over several decades. Some senior members who were involved in the program for over forty years say that they continue to stay engaged because there are no other volunteers to take over their roles, and they still believe in the program. It follows that the level of neighbourhood awareness of Block Parents in a given community was often dependent on the individuals running the program and the outreach and relationships they established within the community.

In contemplating what contributed to the Block Parent Program's success, it is clear that the social, cultural, and technological conditions were ideal at the time the program started. In that tragic time when the London, Ontario, community and Jensen family were grieving, the mobilizing of women, schools, police, and community all fell into place. Moreover, while there was much hard work by the Public Affairs Committee of the National Council of Jewish Women, the initial set up was an informal and low-commitment model built around the lifestyle of stay-at-home women and mothers. This was also at a time when women were exploring their potential role as advocates for social change in their communities (Cooper, 1979), when theories of situational crime prevention were influential (Cohen & Felson, 1979), and when communities were becoming partners in crime prevention (O'Malley & Palmer, 1996; Garland, 2001; Johnston & Shearing, 2002). Additionally, the absence of technology, such as social media and smartphones, and the presence of close ties to neighbours helped the program buy-in, particularly in small to mid-size communities. Importantly, the lack of police support and growing liability concerns were the most commonly cited factors for the programs' decline, an issue that continues to have effects on civic engagement today.[59] Responsive changes to the program to address these arising challenges resulted in additional hurdles and security precautions in the form of screenings and checks, including in some cases sex abuse registry checks and fingerprinting with the onus and scrutiny on the prospective Block Parent volunteer.

This was markedly different from the original inception of the program.

Chapter 3

The Fate of Block Parent: Adaptation and Relevance

The changing landscape of the last five decades has had a profound impact on the Block Parent Program. As outlined in the previous chapter, there were many reasons for these changes: the rescinding of support by police forces, concerns (including financial) about police checks of all household members over twelve years old, concerns about the signs getting into the wrong hands, a fundamental change for women in the workforce that resulted in fewer people at home to volunteer, and a lack of interest in or time for volunteering.

Despite these shifts, the perception of safety offered by Block Parent neighbourhoods continues to have an impact on those who recall using the program or who had parents that volunteered. There have been numerous calls to bring back the Block Parent Program by residents in communities across Canada because of child safety issues – not solely fears about child abduction, but rather, to protect young people from being bullied. For example, a group of citizens in Riverview, New Brunswick, are one community of many who wish to revive the Block Parent Program. One resident recalls that her mother was a Block Parent in the 1980s and would like to be a "second-generation" Block Parent due to concerns about bullying in her area.[1] In Hamilton, Ontario, a Facebook group has been started to bring back the Block Parent Program due to worries about a rise in bullying in the area as illustrated by the tragic case of grade nine student Devan Selvey.[2] Selvey died in his mother's arms in October 2019 outside of his high school after he was stabbed by a fellow student. He had been the victim of bullying since the start of the school year and some felt that very little was done to address the issue by school or police authorities. This grief and sense of loss experienced by the community in relation to the failure to protect youth appears to be the context in which mobilization to enact change occurs, fuelling some communities to call for a revival of the Block Parent Program.

Administrators of the program note the steady flow of requests despite the decline of the program overall:

> Every day I receive emails – how can I be involved? … Every week I get an email or several emails wondering if their community has Block Parent, and it saddens me because we cannot set up new programs especially right now in COVID … We get requests all the time. We find that they run better in small communities– bigger locations don't run well because it would be a full time job to keep track of all of the Block Parents.

How do grieving communities deal with loss and what does a community child protection program look like in the current context? Is there a role for community members to volunteer to assist other vulnerable groups? Given the enormous societal changes since the inception of the first Block Parent Program, the model of community involvement would be significantly different. What would active guardianship look like? Has volunteerism and crime prevention taken a different turn due to technology?

In order to understand the relevance of Block Parent in the current context, an online survey of almost 1,300 Canadians was completed in the summer of 2021 using the services of Angus Reid Group, a national opinion-polling organization. The survey was conducted on adults (over eighteen years old) from four main regions of Canada where Block Parent organization activity was active or recently active. These were the provinces of Ontario, Alberta, and British Columbia, as well as Atlantic Canada (Nova Scotia, New Brunswick, PEI, and Newfoundland and Labrador).

Our interest was in understanding whether individuals engage in crime prevention activities (in-person volunteering, online crime prevention involvement, or hypothetically volunteering for a program like Block Parent). We also surveyed respondents regarding their awareness of Neighbourhood Watch and Block Parent programs, and which concerns about crime were relevant in their neighbourhood. To explore if there is still trust in the idea of a *safe* stranger, we asked those who indicated they had children under seventeen years old whether they would allow their child or children to knock on a Block Parent door if they needed help.

Respondents were asked semi-structured and open-ended questions pertaining to neighbourhood cohesion, their perceptions of safety, fear of crime in their neighbourhood, perceptions of neighbourhood diversity, and concerns about child protection. These factors were examined in relation to respondents' willingness to engage in crime prevention, both in-person and online.[3]

Volunteerism and Crime Prevention

It is worthwhile noting that the large majority (92 per cent) of this sample had not volunteered for crime prevention programs in their neighbourhood and 79 per cent were not involved in crime prevention through online membership in crime awareness groups on social media (Facebook, X [formerly Twitter], Instagram).[4] This reinforces the concerns raised by administrators that a lack of volunteers was, in large part, the reason for the decline in the program and is consistent with other survey research in Canada, the US, UK, and certain European nations showing high interest in crime prevention programs but low participation in community-based crime prevention programs (Roberts & Hastings, 2007). When asked why respondents were not able to volunteer in-person (table 1) the most frequent response (36.6 per cent) was that there were no programs running in their neighbourhood or they do not know how to access those programs. Just under one-third (29.6 per cent) of the responses for not volunteering centred on a lack of time, and about one in five (21.7 per cent) respondents considered their neighbourhood to be safe, so there was no need. Very few, roughly 7 per cent of answers, were concerned with financial, health, or security barriers (such as a police check).

The concerns about not knowing where to volunteer or how to get involved and time issues were quite salient issues for survey respondents. Many indicated in their comments that they volunteer in many other kinds of ways, and they only have so much time. As mentioned by one respondent, "I have volunteered in schools and girl guides for a combined thirty years while raising kids and working full time. A person can only do so much."

For the ninety-nine respondents who indicated that they did volunteer for crime prevention programs (eight preferred not to answer) in their neighbourhood (table 2), child protection was cited as the main reason for just under one-third (29.2 per cent) of respondents. A contribution to the community was noted by just over one-quarter (26.7 per cent) of those surveyed. Interestingly, responding to a criminal incident was not a major priority, with just under 5 per cent of respondents indicating this was the motivation for volunteering. This latter point, taken together with the finding that respondents thought their neighbourhood was safe, and therefore, did not need a crime prevention program, is instructive. It appears from these findings that the day-to-day life of community members is not particularly focused on crime issues. Examining the resurgence of Block Parent over the past five decades shows that it becomes a response, and there is a surge of interest, when

Table 1. Reasons for Not Volunteering for In-Person Crime Prevention

Why Do You Not Volunteer for Crime Prevention Programs?		
	Percentage	Number*
No programs in my neighbourhood/Don't know how to get involved	36.6	722
No time: unable to make a long-term commitment, prefer to give money instead of time	29.6	584
No interest/no need: neighbourhood is safe	21.7	429
Barriers: health, financial, don't want to have a police check	6.9	137
Other	5.2	102
Total	100.0	1,974

*Total number is higher than the 1,297 sample since respondents were invited to check all that applied.

tragic events occur. Without infrastructure and dedicated volunteers, it subsides or it never gets off the ground.

It is also worth noting that in this survey, the reasons for volunteering (table 2) are focused on deeper goals such as creating a safe neighbourhood for children, contributing to the community, or supporting a cause. This substantiates the importance of instrumental and emotional goals of community crime prevention programs (Freiberg, 2001; Sutton et al., 2021) revealing an interest in a guardianship role along with community solidarity.

Many respondents indicated in their comments that they had worked with "Watch" programs like Neighbourhood Watch and Block Parent in the past. Respondents also reported working with policing agencies in different capacities where they could use their job skills to assist with local neighbourhood crime prevention. In addition, comments were provided on other kinds of volunteerism, which focused on broader social and infrastructural perspectives and safety. For example, respondents indicated they worked in homeless shelters, youth centres, Scouts, and traffic safety initiatives. One respondent noted the variety of work they engaged in related to the broad area of crime prevention:

I'm a volunteer with [X] neighbourhood committee, which works on numerous issues such as improving bus/transit access for kids so they don't have to walk along the dangerous road to get to school. I also volunteer with [XX] Coalition, an environmental conservation group that is working to protect wilderness areas. We were able to convince the city and the

Table 2. Reasons for Volunteering for In-Person Crime Prevention

What Prompted You to Volunteer for Crime Prevention Programs in Your Neighbourhood?		
	Percentage	Number*
Make neighbourhood safe for children	29.2	81
Contribution to community/support cause	26.7	74
Improve sense of well-being	11.6	32
To use my skills and experiences	9.8	27
Due to a criminal incident	4.7	13
Other	18.0	50
Total	100.0	277

*Total number is higher than the ninety-nine respondents who said they volunteer because respondents were invited to check all that applied.

Nature Conservancy of Canada to create a municipal park ... and we continue to work with them to ensure the park is a safe space, e.g., improving signage since it's easy for people to get lost on the trails.

When considering crime prevention, respondents considered neighbourhood concerns in criminality terms, but also, importantly, from a social and infrastructure development perspective that focused on more general safety concerns as well as crime prevention through environmental design. Respondents cited a number of "disorder" issues that needed to be addressed, such as concerns about transient and homeless populations, mental health and addiction issues, and poverty. The complexity of neighbourhood concerns is informative in considering how community crime prevention programs might operate in the current context.

In determining respondents' awareness of "Watch" programs like Neighbourhood Watch versus child safety programs like Block Parent, results show that those surveyed were more aware of Neighbourhood Watch versus Block Parent but most had heard of both (table 3). Almost 71 per cent of respondents were very/somewhat familiar with Neighbourhood Watch vs. 65 per cent for Block Parent. The awareness of Block Parent is consistent with a decades old study, conducted in 1980, on residential property crime in Thunder Bay, which found that 64 per cent of respondents in Thunder Bay were aware of the Block Parent Program (Worrell & Sparkes, 1983, p. 60). In addition, Roberts & Hastings' (2007) review of crime prevention survey research reports that awareness of Block Parent in was reasonably high in the mid-1980s and 1990s but declined quite substantially in the early 2000s. As noted

Table 3. Awareness of "Watch" or Child Safety Programs in Neighbourhood

	Are You Aware of a Program Called Neighbourhood Watch?		Are You Aware of a Program Called Block Parent?	
	Percentage	Number	Percentage	Number
Very/somewhat familiar	70.8	918	65.1	845
Have only heard of name	24.8	322	20.6	267
Never heard of before today	4.4	57	14.3	185
Total	100.0	1,297	100.0	1,297

in chapter 2, 1980 was a time when Block Parent was quite active and on the upswing, which seems to suggest that despite the program's decline in activity, awareness of the program has persisted quite remarkably over the last four decades.

It is also important to point out that while Neighbourhood Watch and Block Parent are sometimes conflated as being the same thing, they are distinct programs. As reported by one respondent who has been involved in the Block Parent Program for a number of decades:

> Neighbourhood Watch to me was property, Block Parent was people. To me Neighbourhood Watch looks after my property, you keep an eye on my house for me when I am not there, but Block Parent, we look after kids, the seniors, the people that might need help. We don't get involved with property at all.

For those who were unaware of what the Block Parent Program was about, a brief description was provided. Respondents were asked whether or not Block Parent should be revived, and if so, what it might do for their neighbourhood. Of those who answered this question, a large majority (84 per cent) indicated that the program should, in fact, be revived. Further, in asking respondents to determine what Block Parent might do for their neighbourhood (reported in table 4), the majority (33 per cent) indicated that "safety" would be provided for young people in the neighbourhood, once again reinforcing child protection concerns. Over one-quarter of respondents (26.5 per cent) indicated that it would show that the neighbourhood is close knit (community cohesion), and just under one-quarter (22.1 per cent) indicated that Block Parent would deter possible crime from occurring. This belief in a possible deterrent effect of the Block Parent Program echoes back to the inception of the program where there was a widespread belief that Block Parents and

Table 4. What Would Block Parent Do for Your Neighbourhood if Running?

What Would Block Parent Do for Your Neighbourhood?	Percentage	Number
Safety: make young people feel safer in neighbourhood, and to and from school	32.6	558
Community cohesion: show that the neighbourhood is close knit	26.2	449
Deterrence: deter possible crime from occurring	21.8	374
Supervision: provide supervision for young people in the neighbourhood	18.2	312
Other	1.2	21
Total*	100.0	1,714

*Total number is higher than sample since respondents were invited to check all that applied.

the signs were deterring would-be criminals from entering neighbourhoods to lure children or commit break-ins and other property crimes.

In addition to deterrence through Block Parent guardians, Block Parent signs (though dilapidated) continue to be displayed on school grounds and in communities across Canada (see figure 15). The effect of these signs on perceptions of safety, community cohesion, and potential deterrence is unclear. Hollis et al.'s (2013, p. 67) work discusses the fact that guardianship can be an objective process but can also benefit from illusion. This concept of "symbolic guardianship" refers to the potential deterrent impact of signs – warning that a dog lives in the home, police presence signs, or Neighbourhood Watch and Block Parent signs can elicit a feeling of being observed (Hollis et al., 2013).

Some research has shown a small deterrent effect of Neighbourhood Watch and police signage in relation to potential burglars' decision-making in property offences, though this study was conducted as an online simulation (van Sintemaartensdijk et al., 2022). Other research has indicated that fear and perceptions of victimization increase with the presence of signage for lower and middle-income participants (Schultz & Tabanico, 2009), but whether this serves as a deterrent for would-be offenders is unclear.

Parents/Guardians and Trust in Block Parents

We further examined the relevance of the Block Parent approach for those who indicated they were parents/guardians of children/wards under the age of seventeen. One would expect that they may have

Figure 15. Weathered Block Parent Sign at an Elementary School in Vancouver, British Columbia, 2022.
Credit: A. Gladstone.

unique concerns about child safety due to their own experiences. Given the concerns raised by police about the lack of safely of screened volunteers, parents or guardians may not allow their child to use a Block Parent home due to lack of trust.

There were 291 respondents who indicated they had a child/ward under seventeen years of age. In attempting to understand whether they would trust an adult who volunteered for Block Parent to help their child, we asked this subset of respondents if they would allow their child/ward to knock on a Block Parent door if their child was in need of help. Almost all (92.8 per cent) of respondents indicated they would allow their child to knock on a Block Parent door (table 5).

Clearly there is trust, though hypothetical, associated with those who volunteer with the program despite earlier fears about who may "get their hands" on a Block Parent sign for disreputable purposes.

It also worth pointing out that this sample of Canadian respondents generally felt safe in their neighbourhoods, with the majority (68.4 per

Table 5. Would You Allow Your Child/Ward to Access Help from a Block Parent?

For Parents/Guardians, Would You Allow Your Children to Knock on a Block Parent Door for Help?

	Percentage	Number
Yes	92.8	270
No	7.2	21
Total	100.0	291

cent) indicating that crime in their neighbourhood was somewhat/ much lower than the rest of Canada. The kinds of concerns articulated by respondents in this survey were not solely crime issues, but similar to other research (Kohm, 2009; McGarrell et al.,1997) they straddled crime and disorder issues (table 6). For example, a similar proportion of respondents indicated robbery/break-ins were problems (15.3 per cent) as was garbage/litter lying around (14.8 per cent). Just over 10 per cent indicated strangers were a problem and 6.6 per cent worried about people hanging around in the streets. Violent crime was low on the list of concerns (2.8 per cent). The highest percentage of responses indicated that "none of these" items were problems in the neighbourhood. An examination of the comments that respondents provided to indicate which problems were missing from the list revealed their concerns (among others): street racing, speeding, the use of ATVs in the neighbourhood, concerns about homeless people, vehicular break-ins, domestic assault, stalking, and family disputes.

Examining the issues raised from the list in table 6 that are clearly "crime" concerns (robbery/break-ins, drug dealing or use, deliberate damage to property or vehicles, and violent crime) reveals that 39.3 per cent of the total issues in the neighbourhood where the respondent chose from the list provided are "crime" issues. The remainder relate to disorder and perceptions of safety.

Taken as a whole, this survey presents some interesting findings. First, most respondents did not volunteer their time towards crime prevention activities and most did not have major concerns with crime that would motivate them to serve as a guardian for child protection purposes (such as for Block Parent). There was concern about both crime and disorder issues in neighbourhoods, however, many issues which were raised are not within the purview of a Block Parent approach. Yet, paradoxically, child protection was the main reason put forward for those who indicated that they were involved in crime prevention

Table 6. Are Any of the Following Problems in Your Neighbourhood?

Are Any of the Following Problems in Your Neighbourhood? (Check All That Apply.)		
	Percentage	Number
None of these	15.7	436
Robbery/break-ins	14.7	408
Garbage or litter lying around	14.2	395
People using or dealing drugs	11.5	318
Strangers in the neighbourhood that nobody knows	10.3	286
Vandalism and graffiti and other deliberate damage to property & vehicles	10.3	286
People being drunk or rowdy	6.7	185
People hanging around the streets (loitering)	6.6	184
Teen/kids being bullied	3.5	96
Violent crime	2.8	78
Other	3.8	105
Total	100.0	2,777

volunteering, respondents believed that safety, community cohesion, deterrence and supervision might be accomplished through Block Parent. And finally, parents of children under the age of seventeen were not concerned if their child knocked on the door of Block Parent volunteer indicating at least some level of trust, though only hypothetically.

Further analysis of this data reported elsewhere (Varma, 2023) indicates important relationships between volunteering and community cohesion. Knowing one's neighbours seems to have an impact on actual and potential volunteering in crime prevention for both men and women in this survey. Experiencing an incident that made the respondent fearful appeared to predict women's engagement in online/digital applications for crime prevention, and perceiving that one's neighbourhood had *less* crime predicted women's hypothetical involvement in a Block Parent Program – perhaps indicating a greater feeling of safety to engage with one's neighbours for a purpose – in this case crime prevention.

What Could a Block Parent Model Look Like Today?

As argued by Sutton et al. (2021), it is important to understand the symbolic dimensions of crime prevention policies in addition to the instrumental concerns regarding what "works." While the overarching purpose of the Block Parent Program is about child protection (the instrumental), this survey and the analysis of Annual Reports and other materials from the Block Parent Program suggest that the symbolic dimension of community – and community cohesion– might be the reason why Block Parent persists and why there are calls to bring it back. Residents in some communities across Canada are still concerned with child protection issues – less so about stranger danger and child molestation – and now more regarding bullying. Calls to revive the Block Parent Program once again appear to be spurred by tragic events where communities feel they need to do more to protect youth. There is also a desire to bring back a lost conception of community, where members come to each other's aid, and where shared citizenship is fostered (Garland, 2023).

Solutions to day-to-day community concerns, both related to disorder and crime, are nebulous, and respondents to this survey noted in their comments the larger "quality of life" issues that need to be addressed in addition to crime prevention (traffic safety, domestic abuse and family disputes, homelessness). In the pockets of Canadian communities where Block Parent is still running, there has been an evolution in the program, which focuses on other more routine safety concerns and mobilizes different kinds of volunteers, such as the "walking school bus"[5] referred to in chapter 2. Notably, there has also been a continued expansion of the program to include seniors who may have mental health concerns or dementia and may need to be helped if they wander away from their homes. The findings of this survey suggest that Block Parent may still have a purpose in Canadian communities, albeit quite different from the original inception of the program. The findings from this study also reinforce the importance of community, solidarity, and civic engagement as part of the equation in community crime prevention.

Calculating Security: Community, Collective Consciousness, and the Protection of Vulnerable Populations

We live in a world in which we need to share responsibility. It's easy to say "It's not my child, not my community, not my world, not my problem." Then there are those who see the need and respond. I consider those people my heroes.

– Fred Rogers

Collective responsibility, child protection, and civic duty were at the heart of the inception and prolongation of the Block Parent Program, catalyzed when tragedy struck in 1968. The community mobilized and gained enormous traction, bringing to life the largest volunteer-operated child safety program in Canada. What kept the program operating for decades was the tireless work of Block Parent administrators, the cooperation and endorsement of the police, support from schools through education and awareness training, and a workforce of women homemakers who were available during the day. While the model shifted when women began working outside of the home, the persistence of the program was based upon instrumental concerns – fears about children in the community and worries about stranger danger that were made more salient when tragedy struck other communities. Grieving families and communities came together in solidarity to establish Block Parent homes across the country.

There was also a widespread belief in deterrence, reinforced through police reporting that child molesters would prey upon unprotected neighbourhoods, despite a lack of evidence to this effect. Having a Block Parent sign up in the window symbolized community solidarity – as mentioned in chapter 1, a "silent warning" that told would-be offenders that the young people of this neighbourhood were protected (Morris, 1976, p. 8).

Annual reports catalogued the impact of the program and provided evidence for the work that was been carried out, as well as illustrated the need for continued funding. A chart cited in a 1990 Annual Report (figure 16) provided records of reported incidents requiring Block Parent assistance, noting that despite the incomplete records, "it is apparent that the many Block Parent volunteers across Canada are offering a valuable service by helping to make our neighbourhoods safer places to live" (Block Parent Program of Canada, 1990, p. 4).

Perceptions of safety were at the core of the program, and while the initial thrust of the program was due to an unspeakable tragedy involving a young boy on his way to school, the actual service provided by Block Parent was much broader. The program was available to anyone who was in distress, including adults in need, as noted in the 6 per cent of incidents shown in 1990 (figure 16). A child feeling frightened or lost or worrying about a suspicious person could be provided with the feeling of security through a Block Parent home. Moreover, administrators of the program even quantified the sense of security, providing rough calculations of the number of hours per year children felt safe in their community.

> If we assume, very conservatively, that each of the approximately 250,000 Block Parent homes across Canada displays the window sign one hour per day, and that each of the 1,039 member communities has three board members working five hour per week, then the Block Parent Program contributes over 91 million hours per year to the safety of children, the sense of security within communities and crime prevention. (Block Parent Program of Canada, 1995, p. 5).

Security calculations were documented in yearly annual reports through the reporting of incidents. As can be seen in figure 16, the main kinds of incidents where Block Parents provided assistance were for "lost/frightened children," which included instances where a child was frightened by an animal. Provinces across the country differed in terms of the safety and security needs of children. For example, as discussed by the Block Parent Associations of the Yukon and Yellowknife, children needed to be safeguarded from extreme weather, winter days when travel to and from school occurs in the dark, and concerns about large, unfriendly, and abandoned dogs (Block Parent Program of Canada, 1990, p. 12). Overall, the main staple of the program was providing help to "sick/injured" children, helping kids who were being bullied or harassed, or even assisting when arguments or quarrels were occurring. Incidents relating to assaults, molestation, or attacks were very rare, and in those circumstances, in addition to filling out an incident report for the Block Parent organization, Block

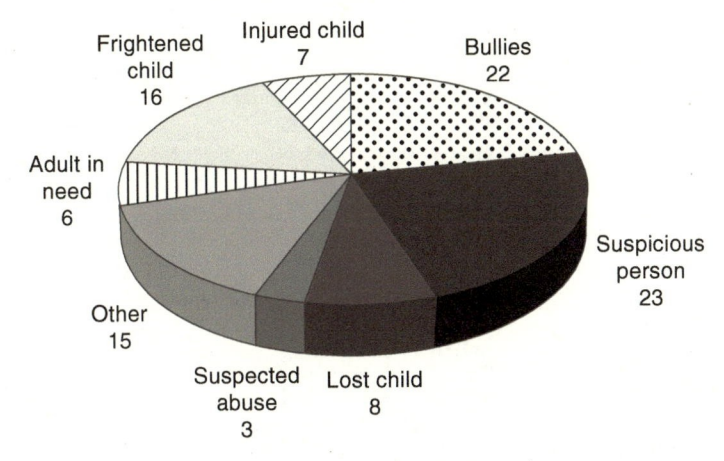

Figure 16. Percentage of Incidents Requiring Assistance of a Block Parent, 1990.

Parents were instructed to keep the child safe and call the police. The essence of the program was more about creating a feeling of safety versus actual incidents and interventions. This posed a challenge for continued funding because it was difficult to quantify a perception of safety in a given community or a possible deterrent effect. As noted by one administrator:

> [The] really difficult thing we come across when we are looking for funding ... how to you count crime prevention? ... So many times you are looking for funding and you get asked, how many clients do you think you are going to service? Or did you have clients coming back afterwards? All talk about clients and numbers. Well, how do you say because I had the sign in the window I prevented maybe a child being picked up in a car, or maybe I prevented bullying, or maybe a senior being lost? You know you can't count it.

The reporting of incidents was incomplete in some years due to some provinces not reporting all incidences and the categories shifting during the years reported. In 2007, due to the retrieval and redistribution of Block Parent window signs, national statistics on incidents were not an accurate representation of actual incidents.

Figure 17 provides the information that was reported in each Annual Report by year (though is limited in accuracy due to the abovementioned issues).

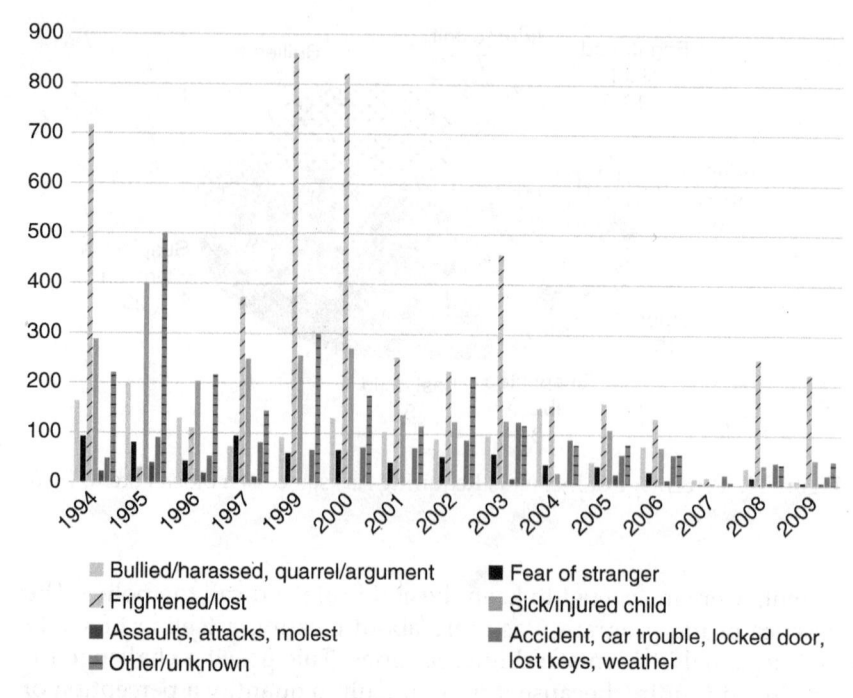

Figure 17. Incidents Requiring the Assistance of a Block Parent, 1994–2009.
Notes: 1990–3 Annual Reports did not provide the raw numbers of incidents. The dissemination of incidents ended as of 2009. The number of Block Parents and Communities was declining during this period and therefore numbers of incidents were declining as well.
Source: Block Parent Program of Canada Annual Reports (1990–2016).

Lost Children's Booths

It is interesting to note that for a four year period (between 2001 and 2004) during the time that Block Parent was seeing a decline in funding, police support, and volunteers, the incidents officially reported in Annual Reports began to include what were called "Lost Children's Booths" as well as "Child Identification Clinics" and "Safe Shelter at Fairs."[1] These booths or tents with Block Parent volunteers were set up at fairs and other large gatherings in case parents or guardians became separated from their children. Most of these booths operated out of the Quebec Block Parent Program. Also part of the Block Parent Program were "Child Identification Clinics," where children's fingerprints and DNA samples were taken and recorded. These clinics would also be

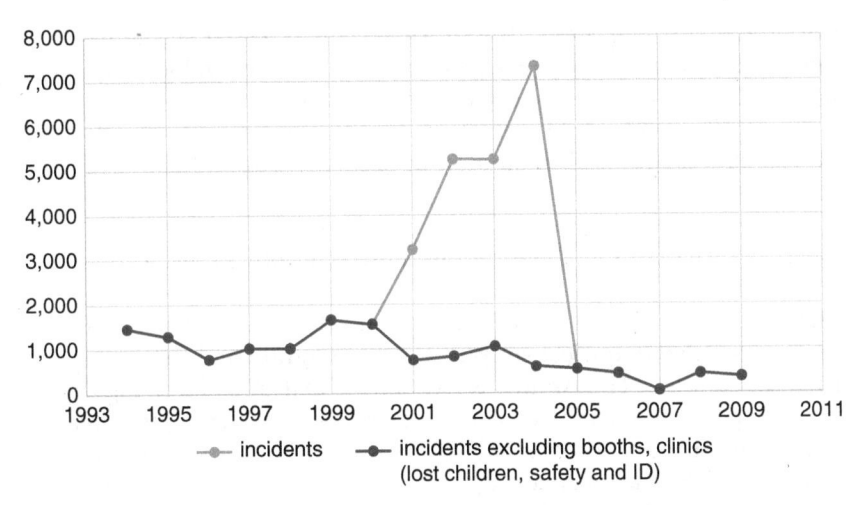

Figure 18. Number of Incidents Requiring Block Parent Assistance.
Notes: 1990–3 Annual Reports did not provide the raw numbers of incidents so figure 18 begins with 1994. The dissemination of incidents ended as of 2009.
Source: Block Parent Program of Canada Annual Reports (1990–2016).

set up at malls so that in the awful event that a child went missing, the parent would have information on the child that could be quickly provided to police. Child Identification Clinics were sponsored by businesses such as Kodak, and support was provided by the RCMP. While these activities were staffed by Block Parent volunteers, this was different from the normal *safe haven* neighbourhood model of the original Block Parent Program. In the incident reports of 2001 and 2004, the official reporting of yearly incidents included these children helped in Lost Booths, dramatically increasing the yearly incident tally.

Figure 18 shows incidents including and excluding Lost Child Booths and Identification Clinics. Perhaps the inclusion of these incident numbers is in response to a program in decline at the time and a desperate need for funding and support. As earlier noted, quantifying the prevention of bullying or assaults or computing the perception of security for the purposes of funding is next to impossible. In any event, the Annual Reports stopped including the Booths and Clinics in calculation of incidents in 2005 and resumed normal incident reports until all reporting of incidents, communities, and homes ceased in 2009 due to a lack of reporting by volunteers and lack of administrative help.

The reporting of incidents was incomplete in some years due to some provinces not reporting all incidences and the categories shifting during the years reported. In 2007, due to the retrieval and redistribu-tion of Block Parent window signs, national statistics on incidents were not an accurate representation of actual incidents.

Figure 18 provides the information that was reported in each Annual Report by year (though is limited in accuracy due to the abovemen-tioned issues).

Security Calculations, Celebrations, and Symbolic Boundaries

The calculation of safety hours, along with the documentation of inci-dents, provided empirical support for the program and reinforced the need for funding. The Annual Reports were instrumental in highlight-ing the operationalization of safe refuge across the country, the breadth and depth of the kinds of incidents that could be handled by the pro-gram, and the value of civic engagement and guardianship in the Block Parent community.

There was also a symbolic dimension to these reports. The Annual Re-ports, activities, recognition of volunteers, and yearly themes were sym-bolic statements about the way society sees its present, past, and future (Sutton et al., 2021, p. 137), binding members of society together under a common purpose (Durkheim, 1984). For Block Parent, the focus on child protection solidified the communities' affirmation of child safety as well as the traditional role of maternal, and later, parental protection and the role of the community in assisting those who are vulnerable.

The community of guardianship was reinforced nationally through the Block Parent organization, and local communities were reinvigor-ated to work together under the common purpose of child protection and safe havens anywhere and everywhere. Further, as noted by Co-hen, the interactions within the community encapsulated the percep-tion of its boundaries (Cohen, 1985, p. 13–14). For Block Parent, while there were physical boundaries in the sense of local communities run-ning the program, provincial programs, and the national organization, the community as a whole became symbolic of protection for children and perceptions of safety. The boundaries that were emblematic of this community were found between the guardians/women of the commu-nity (Block Parents), those that were vulnerable (children, seniors, and others in need), and those that were to be kept out of the community through Block Parent signs and a watchful eye (potential criminals).

Community Well-Being and Finding Purpose

The inception, cultivation, and evolution of the Block Parent Program illustrates the way in which grief and fear mobilized a community, a social movement, and a national program in the space of roughly five decades. As discussed in chapter 1, the conditions for mobilization aligned perfectly. The police, schools, parents, and sponsors – including local businesses – were all on board, and the program spread rapidly to homes and communities across the country. Fear was the driver and child protection the purpose, and while worries about child molesters was the impetus for the program, the actual work involved helping children who were frightened or lost, sick or injured, or felt they were being bullied. Vitally, an attentive and caring volunteer workforce was already in place with women homemakers as guardians of the community. Moreover, criminological theories of situational crime prevention and routine activities theories were having an impact on how to address predatory street crime through a guardianship model, and the additional Block Parent signage was believed to be a deterrent to potential criminal activity. This period of time also coincided with broader societal changes where communities began to have an expanded role in addressing local crime problems, both as "partners" with police and as independent grassroots organizations (O'Malley & Palmer, 1996; Garland, 2001; Johnston & Shearing, 2002; Vallée & Caputo, 2011).

Despite the decline in Block Parent membership and an overall decrease in the number of Canadians who indicate that they volunteer their time, communities are still now seen to be significant partners in identifying the priorities and concerns of crime prevention. The United Nations international standards and norms on crime prevention explicitly highlights the importance of engaging community and civil society in crime prevention initiatives (ECOSOC, 2002, p. 16). In particular, crime prevention should address experiences *beyond* official crime statistics. "Residents and local organizations are fundamental in providing key information on experiences of victimization beyond reported incidents and on perceptions of safety and insecurity" (ICPC, 2008, p. 215). The ICPC notes that perceptions of safety and insecurity are important constructs in crime prevention initiatives – perceptions of safety for children were at the heart of Block Parent.

Child Protection and Community Well-Being

When it comes to safety, security, and experiences of victimization beyond reported incidents, many communities continue to be concerned about the protection of youth, most notably in terms of bullying and child abduction (Melton et al., 2002). Child abduction cases are extremely rare, but the public perceives child abduction involving strangers to be a real and tangible threat to child safety (Pedneault, 2019; Levenson et al., 2007). The moral panic surrounding the danger posed by strangers who abduct children is a powerful mobilizer of legislative and policy change, which focuses on situational crime prevention techniques such as "watch" programs, as well as sex offender residency restrictions, registries, and community notification policies (Durling, 2006). While these programs may serve a symbolic purpose of building community cohesion and providing a perception of safety and deterrence, they also deflect attention away from the more widespread problem of domestic violence and child abuse within families and other state or religious institutions. Despite the need to address these concerns, new solutions to previous fears continue to be put forward, the most recent being a technological solution – the widespread use of Amber Alerts – which have been criticized for being largely ineffectual (Griffin, 2010). In addition to potentially deflecting attention away from the real dangers facing children and youth, the fear of children being abducted by strangers, along with worries about neighbourhood safety, crime, and disorder, has consequences for the well-being and health of communities and their residents (Parsons et al., 2010). For example, parental perceptions on neighbourhood safety, stranger danger, and sociability are associated with children's independent mobility in their neighbourhood. Negative perceptions and fear in parents were associated with less independent mobility of their children (Mitra et al., 2014). Fear has an impact on youth, as well. Youth perceptions of neighbourhood safety and neighbourhood crimes against persons are independently related to their physical activity occurring outside of school (Janssen, 2014).

Bullying is another major child protection concern expressed in public perception surveys (Shelley et al., 2021) and which has an impact on community health and well-being. Peer-to-peer bullying has been shown to have long-term effects on youth in terms of risk for later criminal justice involvement, both as potentials victims and perpetrators (Fergusson et al., 2014), and in terms of numerous mental health concerns including depression, self-harm, and suicidal ideation (Reid, 2010; Schroeder et al., 2011). Research has shown that fear (whether real or unfounded) about child safety and concerns about bullying have long-terms effects on youth both physically and mentally and enormous effects on community and youth well-being. While Block Parent may be considered a model of community crime prevention from a bygone era, the active guardianship and involvement by communities appeared to provide a sense of security to those who needed help though there was no empirical data to support this contention.

From a social development approach, rather than focusing solely on deterrence or displacement of crime, communities may benefit from a rethinking of the concerns they wish to have addressed, which include such issues as family violence and child abuse, mental health, youth homelessness, and unemployment. Addressing these issues may also go further in providing a sense of safety and security to community members as these disorder issues were reported in the survey discussed in chapter 3 as important community concerns.

Guardians of Today

The present-day concern is that we live in a very different world from that of the late 1960s. Most children carry cell phones, many youths do not walk to school, and community members say they do not have time to volunteer (Varma, 2023). In cases where communities are concerned about a specific social issue (like child protection), dimensions of trust among neighbours, community cohesion, civic connection, and neighbourhood support are significant in terms of whether or not community members will engage in active citizenship or engage in volunteering (Farkas & Jones, 2007; Varma, 2023). Two recent Canadian surveys in Toronto (2018) and Toronto's neighbourhood of York (2021) found that most residents had high levels of trust in neighbours, confidence in police, felt safe in their neighbourhoods, and had a strong civic connection with about 40 per cent volunteering their time for the community (Toronto, 2018; Procyk & Dinca-Panaitescu, 2021). However, both surveys noted that these confidence measures varied based upon income, age, race, and the area that residents lived in. Those financially less well off, racialized individuals, and residents in certain neighbourhoods were less engaged than the average. Thus, as noted by Lub (2017) in relation to Neighbourhood Watch, the balance between reducing crime and disorder and social control is a fundamental question. In the name of increased security, some individuals and jurisdictions face increased surveillance and scrutiny, and crime prevention programs thought to be benevolent can cause harm (Welsh & Rocque, 2014). One only needs to recall the tragedy of Trayvon Martin, an innocent and unarmed seventeen-year old African American youth walking in a Florida neighbourhood, who ended up being shot and killed by George Zimmerman, a Neighbourhood Watch community coordinator.[1] Or, the shocking case of fourteen-year-old Brennan Walker, who missed his bus and became lost in a neighbourhood on the way to school. Walker did not have his cell phone with him and ended up knocking on the door of Jeffrey Zeigler, asking for directions, only to be shot at by Zeigler.[2] Tragic cases such as these remind us of the fundamental concerns about community engagement, civic responsibility, and equity in the communities and children who are able to access instrumental outcomes – informal networks and social capital – that may be offered in programs like Block Parent. In addition, there is variation in how communities interact with police and other forms of authority, including the effects on perceptions of safety with signage. Research has indicated that fear and perceptions of victimization *increase* with the presence of signage for lower and middle-income individuals (Schultz & Tabanico, 2009) who may live in communities that need protection. Moreover, newer approaches to crime prevention that occur online may also be subject to problems. Walby and Joshua's (2021) analysis of online crime prevention groups notes that while there is assumed community building and perceptions of safety, there are also concerns about shaming and exaggerating levels of crime, which may serve to increase, rather than decrease, fear in online channels.

Community Well-Being

With these cautions in mind, it is important to note that calls to bring back Block Parent have continued, especially during the COVID-19 pandemic, since more people were working from home. The appeal of the program continues to centre on child safety, but there appears to be more to Block Parent than the sum of its parts. Those who indicate that they want Block Parent reinvigorated also say it brings back a sense of community, where neighbours may once again begin to talk to neighbours. As noted by second-generation Block Parent Anne Bisonnette of New Brunswick, there has been a lot of lingering anxiety after the pandemic, and we need to build community again.[3] This need for community was more salient during the pandemic when lockdowns around the world were isolating people in their homes. To build community, a "hearts in the window" movement spread quickly to show care and provide hope and support for one another.[4] For Jeffrey Moss of Toronto, creating neon hearts saved his lighting business from going under when the pandemic hit and created a new avenue to build community. Customers can order lights in different colours to display in their windows – each signifying support for a different kind of purpose, green for the World Wildlife fund, yellow for the Canadian Cancer Society, and other colours indicating support for local hospitals. According to Moss, "the meaning behind [the hearts] is not only supporting front-line workers, it's also about building community."[5]

The need to build community solidarity and have purpose was at the heart of Block Parent, which fulfilled a societal and individual need. Having a sense of purpose is associated with decreased mortality and increased quality of life (Alimujiang et al., 2019), and volunteering is associated with both physical and mental well-being (Sneed & Cohen, 2013). Religious institutions used to provide the organized machinery for providing purpose and promoting community solidarity. Regarding the functional aspects of religion, McGivern's (2013) discussion of Durkheim notes that religion provides a sense of community, binding people together. This social cohesion, along with a common set of values and collective experience of solidarity that provide meaning and purpose, was necessary for social stability. Moreover, religion offers strength for people during life's transitions and tragedies (McGivern, 2013, p. 475) as did the Block Parent Program for the grieving community in London, Ontario. However, the most recent census data shows that there is a decline in religious affiliation among Canadians and the trend is the same for Americans. More than one-third of Canada's population reported having no religious affiliation or having a secular perspective (atheist, agnostic, humanist, or other secular perspectives), and the proportion of this population has more than doubled in twenty years (Statistics Canada, 2022). Interestingly though, the secular category includes those that have come together in *communities of purpose*. Lori Beaman, professor at the University of Ottawa and the Canada research chair in religious diversity and social change remarks that "we see a kind of openness to come together around things that matter to people, like homelessness, like food banks, like conservation, and so on … So I think that those are the ways that people are finding community in new ways."[6]

Finding Community

Calls for a renewed configuration of Block Parent may build community, contribute to the health and well-being of youth, be useful to an aging or isolated population, and may highlight the broader needs of communities and possible responses from a guardianship-based model. For example, a recent study on social capital in Toronto reported that one out of twelve residents of Toronto had no close family or friends to call for help or talk through their state of mind (Ayer, 2022). This is consistent with a large international survey of thirty-five countries that found that in Ireland, the Netherlands, Switzerland, and Canada over 10 per cent of older adults did not have a spouse or biological child to rely on and were more likely to live alone (Verdery et al., 2019). An organization in the United Kingdom called AgeUK asks neighbours to stop and have chats with the elderly people in their neighbourhood to combat loneliness.[7] And a recent study by the National Institute on Aging even suggested that Canada Post workers may serve a vital role to the elderly, not only delivering the mail but having a "chat and check-in" with seniors on their route (Naylor & Sinha, 2023). There are avenues for a Block Parent guardianship model that centres on community building and help for anyone in distress or who may feel isolated.

The research presented in the book shows that community solidarity may be cultivated through programs like Block Parent and that neighbourhood cohesion and civic engagement may have positive effects on health and well-being. This research also documents the way in which a grieving community, through the advocacy of women on the Public Affairs Committee of the NCJW, created a social movement resulting in a national program lasting over half a decade despite enormous societal and cultural changes.

The impetus for the creation of Block Parent was the tragic death of a young boy on his way to school and the recognition that something had to be done to protect children. The concern, which has been acknowledged by some of the originators of the program, is that Block Parent, if it had been in place, may not have protected Frankie Jensen. Nor is it clear that Block Parent could have changed the outcome for any of the devastating cases that followed the Jensen case. The proliferation of a situational crime prevention approach allowed for a response, and it created a symbol that said that children were safe, and this community was united. At the time of its inception in the late 1960s, Block Parent also provided a place of stability in the face of post-war anxieties surrounding the corruptibility of youth, the dangers posed by strangers, and worries about the stability of family as more women were exploring the possibility of work outside of the home. It provided a feeling of protection during a time when systems of youth justice were guided by a guardianship model for children who were neglected, abused, or delinquent – the *parens patriae* model – which was central to the Juvenile Delinquents Act. However, the guardianship ethos translated well for Block Parent as it was based on maternal guardianship, the home as safe haven, and the community as a united front to keep strangers away.

Situational crime prevention made sense for the original structure of Block Parent, but it did not address the greatest concern of the program – the child abductor. Instead, as evidenced by years of incident reports, it addressed other concerns – lost, frightened, sick, or injured children, or kids who were being bullied or harassed – though "knocks on the door" were infrequent overall. Despite the occasional use of Block Parent, the proliferation of the program during the 1970s and 1980s points to the sense of security it offered to the numerous communities and small businesses that signed on. It provided a venue for community to come together under a common purpose and reveals the importance of the symbolic and instrumental dimensions of crime prevention.

The decline of the program, which became much more pronounced in the late 1990s, was a result of societal changes, such as the greater number of women in the workforce, the concomitant lack of volunteers, and children carrying smartphones, which would allow them to be tracked or to call for help if needed. Perhaps, most fundamentally, the mid- to late 1990s were characterized by a preoccupation with liability and risk, which saw the support of traditional partners (most notably police and schools) being withdrawn. Moreover, the Block Parent volunteer themselves became potential offenders who needed to be screened regularly, fingerprinted, and whose information would be stored in a database. The concerns about liability emerged despite the fact that the Block Parent Program did not have any incidents in its decades-long operation in which children were hurt or in any danger in a Block Parent house. Regardless, the very reason for the inception of the Block Parent Program – the child molester –became one of the factors that led to its demise: the potential molester/volunteer using the sign to gain access to a child.

Despite its decline, Block Parent is still recognized widely and continues to operate in small pockets across the country. It has evolved in its purpose and structure but remains an organization dedicated to protecting children and providing safety in communities. While the functional aspects of Block Parent may have shifted, it appears to still hold a place in the minds of those who interacted with it as volunteers, children, and parents providing community cohesion, mutual aid, and shared citizenship for vulnerable people and for a spectrum of quality of life needs.

Notes

Introduction

1 Mothers to fight parking tickets at guardless crossing. (1968, 9 February). *Globe and Mail*, 4.

2 Edwards, P. (2022, February 20). At least three were caught after nine-year-old Frankie Jensen's murder. Was he killed by a fourth? *Toronto Star*, A.10.

3 The words "BLOCK PARENT®" and the BLOCK PARENT® symbol are registered trademarks of BLOCK PARENT® Program of Canada, Inc. All rights reserved. Hereafter, the term "Block Parent" will be used in this publication with recognition of the registered trademark in place.

4 However it has been documented that both sexual and physical abuse occurred in these training schools against children and youth despite the stated intentions of providing a safe and protected environment. See the CBC documentary "Born Bad": https://www.cbc.ca/cbcdocspov/episodes/born-bad

5 It is important to point out that the term "community" is understood in everyday interactions and yet quite elusive when it comes to defining it for social science purposes (Cohen, 1985, p. 11).

6 However, the COVID-19 pandemic required people to work from home, which, incidentally, sparked interest in reigniting Block Parent in some jurisdictions.
   Steeves, S. (2022, August 29). Block Parent program sees revival in interest since start of pandemic. *Global News*. https://globalnews.ca/news/9092439/block-parent-program-revival-pandemic/

Chapter 1

1 Platiel, R. (1968, March 12). Run to the house with the BP sign, children in trouble told. *Globe and Mail*.

2 Molesters discouraged: Board requests report on block-parent plan. (1968, March 14). *Globe and Mail*.

3 Council decides no need for plan. (1968, 9 April). *Globe and Mail*.
4 Block Parent was "born of tragedy" (personal communication, S. Siskind, September 5, 2023) but most of the young women who created it went on to work in community health and wellness related fields. Shelly Siskind became a public speaker and author volunteering with children and families with a focus on mental health and self-healing. Gerbrig Berman, a nurse, started a business and co-authored a book with Siskind; Ellen Rosen served as director of Nursing at London Health Sciences Centre; and Arlene Gladstone, MSW served as an executive director of Family Services of the North Shore (Vancouver) and continued her volunteer work with the arts, the Vancouver Police Board, and the Jewish community.
5 Morality Departments existed within Police Forces in the late 1800s in Canadian cities. For example, the Toronto Police Morality Department emerged in the 1880s, tasked with rooting out vice in the city, but according to Marquis (1992) it played an important (but controversial) role in dispute resolution for working-class families and collecting support payments prior to the establishment of family courts in 1929. See Marquis, G. (1992). The police as a social service in early twentieth-century Toronto. *Histoire Social*, 25(50), 335–58.
6 Macrotrends. (2024). *London, Canada metro area population 1950–2024*. https://www.macrotrends.net/cities/20382/london/population
7 Paradoxically, in the mid-2000s police raised concerns about volunteers being a potential risk to a child or young person, despite the police screening.

Chapter 2

1 Waterloo Regional Block Parent Program. (2014). *We need you*. https://blockparents.ca/wpcontent/uploads/2017/01/We-Need-You-2014.pdf
2 Cornacchia, C. (2015, April 21). Block parent makes a comeback in Pointe Claire. https://montrealgazette.com/news/local-news/west-island-gazette/block-parents-makes-a-comeback-in-pointe-claire; British Columbia Crime Prevention Association. (n.d.). *Youth and crime prevention*. https://www.publicsafety.gc.ca/lbrr/archives/cn000013203254-eng.pdf
3 MacIvor, D. (2000, April 7). Block parent program still going strong in rural areas. *Sarnia Observer*.
4 Block-parent idea to be studied to help victims of racial attacks. (1979, April 9). Special to *Globe and Mail*, 16.
5 Block parents asked to help fight incest. (1980, May 10). *Globe and Mail*, 15.
6 Block Parent Program of Winnipeg. (2015). *A Brief history of block parents of Winnipeg*. https://winnipegblockparents.mb.ca/history/
7 Two outstanding volunteers receive the Therese Casgrain volunteer award during national volunteer week (2003, April 29). *Canada NewsWire*.

8 Lily Schreyer Block Parent, needed or not. (1980, October 30). *Globe and Mail*, 9; Cuff, J. (1981, September 12). Family, fame, and fortune Ian Thomas hated Woodstock and is a Block Parent. He is also one of Canada's rock and roller. *Globe and Mail*, F7.

9 Hansard. (1982, June 17). Legislative Assembly of Ontario: 32nd Parliament, 2nd Session. https://www.ola.org/en/legislative-business/house-documents/parliament-32/session-2/1982-06-17/hansard

10 Agency, Q. (2015, July 30). Block parents are back. *Cochrane Times*.

11 Carey, A. (1977, September 30). Neighbours keep their doors open. *Toronto Star*. Section D; Tivy, P. (1989, October 23). Partying pumpkin is guest of honor at candy fest. *Calgary Herald*.

12 Galloway, G. (2009, January 5). Block parent marker vanishing from homes across the country. *Globe and Mail*.

13 Latch-key children need help: Report. (1982, December 2). *Globe and Mail*.

14 Teahan, K. (1985, September 2). After-school programs the real key for kids to latch on to. *Globe and Mail*.

15 Bell, S. (1993, January 23). Citizens take the crime fight into their own hands. *Vancouver Sun*.

16 Scotton, L. (1990, November 8). Murder of Andrea Atkinson sparks renewed interest in block parent program safe haven. *Toronto Star*.

17 Bell, S. (1993, January 23).

18 Kilfoyle, H. (1985, November 4). Block parents come to the country to protect rural children. *Kingston Whig Standard*.
    MacIvor, D. (2000, April 7). Block parent program still going strong in rural areas: Final edition. *Sarnia Observer*; Bell, S. (1993, January 23).

19 Scotton, L. (1990, November 8).

20 Province of Manitoba. (n.d.). *Sex offender notifications: Purpose of making community notification*. Justice. https://www.gov.mb.ca/justice/commsafe/notification/index.html

21 Cole, T. (1999, January 25). Community on patrol parents help police cut crime. *Daily Gleaner* (New Brunswick).

22 Cole, T. (1999, January 25).

23 Stirling, C. (2005, February 24). Block parent enters a new era. *Calgary Herald*.

24 Collins, W. (2000, October 27). Block parents are hoping to recruit more members for the community programme; help when needed. *Guelph Daily Mercury*.

25 MacIvor, D. (2000, April 7). Block parent program still going strong in rural areas: Final edition. *Sarnia Observer*.

26 MacIvor, D. (2000).

27 Collins, W. (2000, October 27).

28 Winnipeg Block Parents. (n.d.). *Block parent homes in Winnipeg*. https://www.winnipegblockparents.mb.ca/BPhomes.html

29 Block Parent Program of Winnipeg. (n.d.). *Trusty's Page*. https://winnipegblockparents.mb.ca/bear/

30 North Point Douglas Women's Centre. (n.d.). *Mama Bear Clan*. https://www.npdwc.org/mama-bear-clan

31 Summit New Service. (2001, March 7). Local block parent volunteer facing charges of fraud over $5,000. *New Brunswick Telegraph Journal*; Times Globe. (2001, March 21). Treasurer admits to stealing thousands from block parent association. *New Brunswick Telegraph Journal*; NB block parent treasurer who stole $38,000 sentenced to house arrest. (2001, April 19). *Canadian Press NewsWire*.

32 Anticrime activities funded. (2002, July 18). *Whitehorse Daily Star*.

33 Abbate, G. (2002, June 8). Block parents: Is anybody home? On the mean streets of the megacity, much-needed volunteers are few and far between. *Globe and Mail*.

34 Martin, E. (2002, July 31). Get involved in block parents to protect children. *Sault Star*.

35 McGinn, D. (2013, October 28). How the 21st century put the Block Parent program into decline. *Globe and Mail*.
    Derbyshire, M. (2006, August 5). Block Parents not welcome; organization left York after police pulled support. *Era Banner*, Newmarket.

36 Ritchie, K. (2003, June 23). The Disappearance of the Block Parent. *Ottawa Citizen*.

37 Derbyshire, M. (2006, August 5).

38 Beutel, T. (2003, October 15). Back on the block: Child safety program has new life. *Richmond News* (BC).

39 Ritchie, K. (2003, June 23).

40 Mettrick, A. (2003, January 30). Block parents to be fingerprinted. *Daily News* (Prince Rupert, BC).

41 Childs, N. (2003 April 7). Block Parent Program still safe in Brantford. *Brantford Expositor*.

42 Beutel, T. (2003, October 15).

43 Yourk, D. (2003). Cecilia reward grows. *Globe and Mail*.

44 Medals for Block Parents. (2003, January 14). *Telegraph Journal* (New Brunswick).

45 Riley, M. (2007, October 5). Block Parent lacks enough volunteers to keep going. MyKawartha.com. https://www.mykawartha.com/news-story/3696305-block-parent-lacks-enough-volunteers-to-keep-going/.

46 Horner, N. (2005, February 25). Block Parents close doors. *Parksville, Qualicum News* (British Columbia).

47 Derbyshire, M. (2006, August 5).

48 Derbyshire, M. (2006, August 5).

49 Derbyshire, M. (2006, August 5).

50 "Medium-Low" risk implies that risk events have occurred in the past and are likely to occur in the future with a negligible to measureable impact to day-to-day operations (RCMP, 2006, ii footnote).

51 Trick-or-treat safety tips. (2006, October 31). *Winnipeg Free Press*.

52 Galloway, G. (2009, January 5).

53 Community rallies to find missing Ontario girl; Many frustrated that police won't issue Amber Alert. (2009, April 11). *Telegraph-Journal* (Saint-John, New Brunswick).

54 Horner, N. (2005, February 25). Block parents close doors. *Parksville, Qualicum News* (British Columbia).

55 Galloway, G. (2009, January 5).

56 Reader To Reader Column. (2012, September 29). *London Free Press*.

57 Brenk, D. (2016, November 8). London Block Parents closing doors for good. *London Free Press*.

58 Bridge, T. (2019). Block Parent Program signs off in Stratford. *Beacon Herald* (Stratford).

59 Taylor, P.S. (2023, November 30). Opinion: Excessively onerous police checks are killing volunteering. *Financial Post Comment*. https://financialpost.com /opinion/excessively-onerous-police-checks-killing-volunteering

Chapter 3

1 Steeves, S. (2022, August 29). Block Parent program sees revival in interest since start of pandemic. *Global News*.

2 Hristova, B. (2020, February 26). Calls for revival of Hamilton Block Parent program amid anti school-bullying campaign. *CBC News* (Hamilton).

3 for more details see Varma, K. (2023). Volunteering for community crime prevention: Examining guardianship and the Block Parent Program of Canada. *Crime Prevention and Community Safety*, 25(3), 258–81.

4 In contrast, the most recent data from Statistics Canada (2021) indicates that 79 per cent of Canadians over fifteen years of age indicated that they engaged in volunteer work (both formal, mediated through organizations, and informal, without the involvement of an organization or group). However, this percentage includes *all forms* of volunteering, not just crime prevention as was asked of respondents in this survey. https://www150 .statcan.gc.ca/n1/pub/75-006-x/2021001/article/00002-eng.htm

5 Mondou, T. (2016, 19 October). Parents can rest easy with Walking School Bus. https://www.cambridgetimes.ca/opinion/columnists/parents-can -rest-easy-with-walking-schoolbus/article_20d30fc7-6fc7-5b40-a811-5ce99 fd8ea64.html

Chapter 4

1 Not shown in figure 15.

Conclusion

1 Alvarez, L., & Buckley, C. (2013, July 13). Zimmerman is acquitted in Trayvon Martin killing. *New York Times.* https://www.nytimes.com/2013/07/14/us/george-zimmerman-verdict-trayvon-martin.html

2 Wimbley, R., & Komer, D. (2023, February 18). Man who shot at lost Black teen who knocked at his door, gets early parole. *Fox2Detroit.* https://www.fox2detroit.com/news/man-who-shot-at-lost-black-teen-who-knocked-on-his-door-gets-early-parole

3 Steeves, S. (2022, August 29). Block Parent program sees revival in interest since start of pandemic. *Global News.* https://globalnews.ca/news/9092439/block-parent-program-revival-pandemic/

4 Wiechel, A. (2020, March 20). "Hearts in the window" movement spreads warmth, reassurance in the time of COVID-19. *CTV News* (Vancouver). https://bc.ctvnews.ca/hearts-in-the-window-movement-spreads-warmthreassurance-in-the-time-of-covid-19-1.4867029

   Ibrahimji, A. (2020, March 26). People are decorating their windows with hearts and messages of hope right now.

   CNN. https://www.cnn.com/2020/03/26/world/window-hope-messages-trnd/index.html

5 Popoff, T. (2021, March 29). *The story behind these neon lights popping up all over Toronto.* Streets of Toronto. https://streetsoftoronto.com/neon-hearts-toronto/

6 Thompson, N. (2022, October 27). More Canadians than ever have no religious affiliation, census shows. *CBC News.* https://www.cbc.ca/news/canada/kitchener-waterloo/canadian-census-religious-affiliation-none-1.6631293

7 AgeUK. (2019, February 11). More than 3m older people rely on friendly neighbours to brighten up their days. https://www.ageuk.org.uk/latest-press/articles/2019/february/older-people-rely-on-neighbours/

References

Adams, M.L. (1995). Youth, corruptibility, and English-Canadian postwar campaigns against indecency, 1948-1955. *Journal of the History of Sexuality*, 6(1), 89–117. https://www.jstor.org/stable/3704439

Alimujiang, A., Wiensch, A., Boss, J., & Fleischer, N.L. (2019). Association between life purpose and mortality among US adults older than 50 years. *American Medical Association*, 2(5), e194270. https://doi.org/10.1001/jamanetworkopen.2019.4270

Arntfield, M. (2015). *Murder City: The untold story of Canada's serial killer capital. 1959–1984.* Friesen Press.

Ayer, S. (2022). *Toronto Foundation and the Environics Institute for Survey Research Toronto social capital study.* https://www.environicsinstitute.org/projects/project-details/toronto-social-capital-study-2022

Block Parent Program of Winnipeg. (n.d.). *Trusty's Page.* https://winnipegblockparents.mb.ca/bear/

Block Parent Program of Canada Inc. (1983). *Official motions book* [unpublished source].

Braithwaite, J. (2000). Repentance rituals and restorative justice. *The Journal of Political Philosophy*, 8(1), 115–31. https://doi.org/10.1111/1467-9760.00095

Brantingham, P.L., & Brantingham, P.J. (1993). Environment, routine, and situation: towards a pattern theory of crime. In R.V. Clarke & M. Felson (Eds.), *Routine activity and rational choice: Advances in criminological theory* (Vol. 5, pp. 259–94). Routledge.

Bjornstrom, E.E. (2011). The neighborhood context of relative position, trust, and self-rated health. *Soc Sci Med*, 73(1), 42–9. https://doi.org/10.1016/j.socscimed.2011.05.014

Block Parent Program of Winnipeg. (2015). *A brief history of block parents of Winnipeg.* https://winnipegblockparents.mb.ca/history/

Bouffard, J.A., & LaQuana N.A. (2019). Time-series analyses of the impact of sex offender registration and notification law implementation and subsequent modifications on rates of sexual offences. *Crime & Delinquency*, *65*(11), 1483–512. https://doi.org/10.1177/0011128717722010

Chunn, D.E. (1992). *From punishment to doing good: Family courts and socialized justice in Ontario 1880–1940*. University of Toronto Press.

Cohen, A.P. (1985). *Symbolic construction of community*. Routledge. https://doi.org/10.4324/9780203131688

Cohen, L.E., & Felson, M. (1979). Social change and crime rate trends: A routine activity approach. *American Sociological Review*, *44*(4), 588–608. https://doi.org/10.2307/2094589

Cooper, P. (1979). Women as advocates in their communities. *Atlantis*, *4*(2), 121–7. https://atlantisjournal.ca/index.php/atlantis/article/view/4746/3976

Durkheim E. (1984). *The division of labor in society* (W.D. Halls & L.A. Coser, Trans.). Free Press.

Durkheim E. (1986). The elementary forms of religious life. In R.A. Jones (Ed.), *Emile Durkheim: An introduction to four major works* (pp. 115–55). Sage. (Original work published 1912)

Durling, C. (2006). Never going home: Does it make us safer? Does it make sense? Sex offenders, residency restrictions, and reforming risk management law. *Journal of Criminal Law and Criminology*, *97*(1), 317–63. https://scholarlycommons.law.northwestern.edu/cgi/viewcontent.cgi?article=7257&context=jclc&httpsredir=1

Farkas, M., & Jones R. (2007). Community partners: "Doing doors" as a community crime prevention strategy. *Criminal Justice Studies*, *20*(3), 295–312. https://doi.org/10.1080/14786010701617698

Fergusson, D.M., Boden J., & and Horwood, L. (2014). Bullying in childhood, externalizing behaviors, and adult offending: Evidence from a 30-year study. *Journal of School Violence*, *13*(1), 146–64. https://doi.org/10.1080/15388220.2013.840642

Fosarelli, P. (1984). Latchkey children. *Developmental and Behavioral Pediatrics*, *5*(4), 173–7. https://doi.org/10.1097/00004703-198408000-00003

Freiberg, A. (2001). Affective versus effective justice: Instrumentalism and emotionalism in criminal justice. *Punishment and Society*, *3*(2), 265–78. https://doi.org/10.1177/14624740122228320

Fox, R.G. (1984). "The treatment of juveniles in Canadian criminal law." In A.N. Doob & E.L. Greenspan (Eds.), *Perspectives in criminal law: Essays in honour of John Ll. J. Edwards* (pp. 149–85). Canada Law Book.

Garland, D. (2001). *The culture of control: crime and social order in contemporary society*. University of Chicago Press.

Garland, D. (2023). The current crisis of American criminal justice: A structural analysis. *Annual Review of Criminology*, *6*(1), 43–63. https://doi.org/10.1146/annurev-criminol-030722-035139

Goffman, E. (1959). *The presentation of self in everyday life*. Bantam Doubleday Dell.

Griffin, T. (2010). An empirical examination of AMBER Alert "successes." *Journal of Criminal Justice, 38*(5), 1053–62. https://doi.org/10.1016/j.jcrimjus.2010.07.008

Hastings, Ross. (2005). Perspectives on crime prevention: Issues and challenges. *Canadian Journal of Criminology and Criminal Justice, 47*(2), 209–20. https://doi.org/10.3138/cjccj.47.2.209

Heidinger, L. (2002). Profile of Canadians who experienced victimization during childhood, 2018. *Juristat, 85-002-X*. https://www150.statcan.gc.ca/n1/pub/85-002-x/2022001/article/00016-eng.htm

Hollis, M.E., Felson, M., & Welsh, B.C. (2013). The capable guardian in routine activities theory: A theoretical and conceptual reappraisal. *Crime Prevention and Community Safety, 15*(1), 65–79. https://doi.org/10.1057/cpcs.2012.14

Hollis, M.E., Fenimore, D.M., Caballero, M., & Hankhouse, S. (2019). Examining guardianship in action in Waco, Texas. *Crime Prevention and Community Safety, 21*(1), 68–80. https://doi.org/10.1057/s41300-018-0056-5

Hunter, A. (1985). Private, parochial, and public social orders: The problem of crime and incivility in urban communities. In G.D. Suttles & M.N. Zald (Eds.), *The challenge of social control: Institution building and systemic constraint* (pp. 230–42). ABLEX.

Iacovetta, F. (1999). Gossip, contest, and power in the making of suburban bad girls: Toronto, 1945-60. *The Canadian Historical Review, 80*(4), 585–624. https://doi.org/10.3138/CHR.80.4.585

Janssen, I. (2014). Crime and perceptions of safety in the home neighborhood are independently associated with physical activity among 11–15 year olds. *Preventive Medicine, 66*, 113–17. https://doi.org/10.1016/j.ypmed.2014.06.016

Johnston, L., & Shearing, C.D. (2002). *Governing security: Explorations of policing and justice* (1st ed.). Routledge. https://doi.org/10.4324/9780203350713

Karibo, H. (2008). "Now is the time to fight": Juvenile delinquency, drug addiction, and the construction of a moral program in postwar Toronto, 1945-1960. *Social History of Alcohol and Drugs, 22*(2), 262–85. https://doi.org/10.1086/22020262

Kohm, S.A. (2009). Spatial dimensions of fear in a high-crime community: Fear of crime or fear of disorder? *Canadian Journal of Criminology and Criminal Justice, 51*(1), 130. https://doi.org/10.3138/cjccj.51.1.1

Kubrin, C.E., Branic, N., & Hipp, J.R. (2021). (Re)conceptualizing neighborhood ecology in social disorganization theory: From a variable-centered approach to a neighborhood-centered approach. *Crime & Delinquency, 68*(11), 2008–32. https://doi.org/10.1177/00111287211041527

Lansdowne Technologies Inc. (2006, October 26). *Block Parent program risk assessment: Final report*. Prepared for The Royal Canadian Mounted Police.

Levenson, J.S., Brannon, Y.N., Fortney, T., & Baker, J. (2007). Public perceptions about sex offenders and community protection policies. *Analyses of Social Issues and Public Policy, 7*(1), 137–61. https://doi.org/10.1111/j.1530 -2415.2007.00119.x

Lub, V. (2017). Neighbourhood watch: Mechanisms and moral implication. *British Journal of Criminology, 58*(4), 906–24. https://doi.org/10.1093/bjc/azx058

Macrotrends. (2024). *London, Canada metro area population 1950–2024.* https:// www.macrotrends.net/cities/20382/london/population

Marquis, G. (1992). The police as a social service in early twentieth-century Toronto. *Histoire Social, 25*(50), 335–58. https://hssh.journals.yorku.ca /index.php/hssh/article/view/16474

Mawby, R. (2019). *Volunteering: Variations within the criminal justice system.* [Unpublished manuscript].

McGarrell, E. Giacomazzi A., & Q. Thurman (1997). Neighborhood disorder, integration, and the fear of crime. *Justice Quarterly, 14*(3), 479–500. https:// doi.org/10.1080/07418829700093441

McGivern, R. (2013). Religion. In W. Little, & R. McGivern (Eds.). *Introduction to sociology* (1st Canadian ed). OpenStax College.

Melton, G. (editor), Thompson, R., & Small, M. (2002*). Toward a child-centered, neighborhood-based child protection system: A report of the Consortium on Children, Families, and the Law.* Praeger.

Milan, A. (2015). *Women in Canada: A gender-based statistical report* (Catalogue no. 89-503-X). Minister of Industry. https://www150.statcan.gc.ca/n1/pub /89-503-x/2015001/article/14152-eng.htm

Mitra, R., Faulkner, G., Buliung, R., & Stone, M. (2014). Do parental perceptions of the neighbourhood environment influence children's independent mobility? Evidence from Toronto, Canada. *Urban Studies, 51*(16), 3401–19. https://doi.org/10.1177/0042098013519140

Morris, E. (1976). Protecting the kids in your neighbourhood. *Homemakers, 11*(1). Comac Communications.

Myers, T. (2021). The voluntary delinquent: Parents, daughters, and the Montreal juvenile delinquents' court in 1918. *The Canadian Historical Review, 102*(s3), 675–97. https://doi.org/10.3138/chr-102-s3-007

Naylor S., and S.K. Sinha (2023). *Special delivery: How Canadian postal workers could better enable ageing in the right place.* National Institute on Ageing, Toronto Metropolitan University.

O'Malley, A. (2023). *A crisis of innocence: Comic books and children's culture, 1940–1954.* https://crisisofinnocence.library.torontomu.ca/

O'Malley, P. (Ed.). (2006). *Governing risks* (1st ed.). Routledge. https://doi.org /10.4324/9781315253893

O'Malley, P., & Palmer, D. (1996). Post-Keynesian Policing. *Economy and Society, 25*(2), 137–55. https://doi.org/10.1080/03085149600000007

Parnaby, P.F. (2006). Crime prevention through environmental design: Discourses of risk, social control, and a neo-liberal context. *Canadian Journal of Criminology and Criminal Justice, 48*(1), 1–30. https://doi.org/10.3138/cjccj.48.1.1

Parsons, J.A., Singh, G., Scott, A.N., Nisenbaum, R., Balasubramaniam, P., Jabbar, A., Zaidi, Q., Sheppard, A., Ramsay, J., O'Campo, P., & Dunn, J. (2010). Standardized observation of neighbourhood disorder: Does it work in Canada? *International Journal of Health Geography, 9*, 6. https://doi.org/10.1186/1476-072X-9-6

Pedneault, A. (2019). Public (mis)perceptions of individuals who sexually abuse children and the implications thereof. In I. Bryce, Y. Robinson, & W. Petherick (Eds.), *Child abuse and neglect: Forensic issues in evidence, impact, and management* (pp. 419–33). Elsevier Academic Press. https://doi.org/10.1016/B978-0-12-815344-4.00022-2

Pinker, S. (2014). *The village effect: How face-to-face contact can make us healthier, happier, and smarter* (1st ed.). Spiegel and Grau.

Platt, A. (1977). *The child savers: The invention of delinquency* (2nd ed.). University of Chicago Press.

Procyk, S., & Dinca-Panaitescu, M. (2021). *York Region social capital Study.* https://www.unitedwaygt.org/wp-content/uploads/2021/10/York_Social_Capital_Report_2021_Online.pdf

Province of Manitoba. (n.d.). *Sex offender notifications: Purpose of making community notification.* Justice. https://www.gov.mb.ca/justice/commsafe/notification/index.html

Reeves, J. (2012). If you see something, say something: Lateral surveillance and the uses of responsibility. *Surveillance & Society, 10*(3/4), 235–48. https://doi.org/10.24908/ss.v10i3/4.4209

Reid, S.A. (2010). The untapped potential in our communities to assist youth engaged in risky behaviour. *International Journal of Child, Youth and Family Studies, 1*(2), 179–203. https://doi.org/10.18357/ijcyfs122010686

Reynald, D. (2010). Guardians on guardianship: Factors affecting the willingness to supervise, the ability to detect potential offenders, and the willingness to intervene. *Journal of Research in Crime and Delinquency, 47*(3), 358–90. https://doi.org/10.1177/0022427810365904

Roberts, J.V., Hastings, R. (2007). Public opinion and crime prevention: A review of international findings. *IPC Review, 1*, 193–218. https://www.publicsafety.gc.ca/lbrr/archives/cnmcs-plcng/ripcr-v1-193-218-eng.pdf

Rossner, M. (2019). Restorative justice, anger, and the transformative energy of forgiveness. *The International Journal of Restorative Justice, 2*(3), 368–88. https://doi.org/10.5553/IJRJ.000005

Rossner, M., & Meher, M. (2014). Emotions in ritual theories. In Jan E. Stets & J.H. Turner (Eds.), *Handbooks of sociology and social research: Vol. 2. Handbook of the sociology of emotions* (pp. 199–220). Springer Netherlands.

Rothman, D.J. (1980). *Conscience and convenience: The asylum and its alternatives in progressive America*. Little, Brown.

Sampson R.J., Raudenbush, S.W., & Earls, F. (1997). Neighborhoods and violent crime: A multilevel study of collective efficacy. *Science, 277*(5328), 918–24. https://doi.org/10.1126/science.277.5328.918

Schultz, P.W., & Tabanico, J.J. (2009). Criminal beware: A social norms perspective on posting public warning signs. *Criminology, 47*(4), 1201–22. https://doi.org/10.1111/j.1745-9125.2009.00173.x

Shaw, C.R., & McKay, H.D. (1942). *Juvenile delinquency and urban areas*. University of Chicago Press.

Sutton, A., Cherney, A., White, R., & Clancey, G. (2021). *Crime prevention: Principles, perspectives, practices* (3rd ed.). Cambridge University Press.

Schneider, S. (2007). Refocusing crime prevention: Collective action and the quest for community. University of Toronto Press.

Schroeder, B., Messina, M., Schroeder, D., Good, K., Barto, S., Saylor, J., & Masiello, M. (2011). The implementation of a statewide bullying prevention program: Preliminary findings from the field and the importance of coalitions. *Health Promotion Practice, 13*(4), 489–95. https://doi.org/10.1177/1524839910386887

Shelley, W., Pickett, J., Mancini, C., McDougle, R., Rissler, G., & Clearly, H. (2017). Race, bullying, and public perceptions of school and university safety. *Journal of Interpersonal Violence, 36*(1–2). https://doi.org/10.1177/0886260517736272

Simon, J. (1995). Power without parents: Juvenile justice in a postmodern society. *Cardozo Law Review, 16*(3–4), 1363–425. Ayer, S. (2022). *Toronto Foundation and the Environics Institute for Survey Research Toronto social capital study*. https://www.environicsinstitute.org/projects/project-details/toronto-social-capital-study-2022

Sneed, R.S., & Cohen, S. (2013). A prospective study of volunteerism and hypertension risk in older adults. *Psychology and Aging, 28*(2), 578–86. https://doi.org/10.1037/a0032718

Taveggia, T., & Thomas, E.M. (1974). Latchkey children. *The Pacific Sociological Review, 17*(1), 27–34. University of California Press. https://doi.org/10.2307/1388595

Toronto Foundation and the Environics Institute for Survey Research. (2008). *Toronto Social Capital Study*. https://www.environicsinstitute.org/docs/default-source/project-documents/toronto-social-capital-project/toronto-social-capital-study---final-report.pdf?sfvrsn=4ff43083_2

Trépanier, J. (1999). Juvenile courts after 100 years: Past and present orientations. *European Journal on Criminal Policy and Research, 7*(3), 303–27. https://doi.org/10.1023/A:1008780703191

Vallée, M. (2010). Crime prevention and community safety: A conceptual overview. *International Journal of Child, Youth & Family Studies, 1*(1), 1–20. https://doi.org/10.18357/ijcyfs112010171

Vallée, M., & Caputo, T. (2011). *Crime prevention and community safety for children and youth in Canada.* University of Victoria.

van Bavel, M.L. (2019). *Active guardianship, its agents and the effects on offender behavior* [Unpublished PhD thesis]. Faculty of Law, Management and Organisation, Criminology, A-Lab. Vrije Universiteit Amsterdam.

van Sintemaartensdijk, I., van Gelder, J.L., van Prooijen, J.W., Nee, C., Otte, M., & van Lange, P. (2022). Assessing the deterrent effect of symbolic guardianship through neighbourhood watch signs and police signs: A virtual reality study. *Psychology, Crime & Law, 30*(1), 1–21. https://doi.org/10.1080/1068316x.2022.2059480

Varma, K.N. (2023). Volunteering for community crime prevention: Examining guardianship and the Block Parent program of Canada. *Crime Prevention and Community Safety, 25*(3), 258–81. https://doi.org/10.1057/s41300-023-00180-6

Verdery, A.M., Margolis, R., Zhou, Z., Chai, X., & Rittirong, J. (2019). Kinlessness around the world. *The Journals of Gerontology Series B, 74*(8), 1394–405. https://doi.org/10.1093/geronb/gby138

Walby, K., & Joshua, C. (2021). Community crime prevention and crime watch groups as online private policing. *Safer Communities, 20*(4), 237–50. https://doi.org/10.1108/SC-05-2021-0016

Waterloo Regional Block Parent Program. (2014). *We need you.* https://blockparents.ca/wpcontent/uploads/2017/01/We-Need-You-2014.pdf

Welsh, B., & Rocque, M. (2014). When crime prevention harms: A review of systematic reviews. *Journal of Experiential Criminology, 10,* 245–66. https://doi.org/10.1007/s11292-014-9199-2

Winnipeg Block Parents. (n.d.). *Block parent homes in Winnipeg.* https://www.winnipegblockparents.mb.ca/BPhomes.html

Worrell, P.B., & Sparkes, A.T. 1983. *A study of residential crime in Thunder Bay.* National Criminal Justice Reference Service. https://www.ojp.gov/pdffiles1/Digitization/89778NCJRS.pdf

Young, J.L. (2016). G. Stanley Hall, child study, and the American public. *The Journal of Genetic Psychology, 177*(6), 195–208. https://doi.org/10.1080/00221325.2016.1240000

Zevitz, R.G., & Farkas, M.A. (2000). Sex offender community notification: Managing high risk criminals or exacting further vengeance? *Behavioral Sciences & the Law, 18*(2–3), 375–91. https://doi.org/10.1002/1099-0798(200003/06)18:2/3<375::AID-BSL380>3.0.CO;2-N

Legislation and Reports

Block Parent Program of Canada. (1990–2016). *Annual reports.* http://www
.blockparent.ca/areports.htm

B.C. Crime Prevention Association. (1988). *Youth and crime prevention.* https://
www.publicsafety.gc.ca/lbrr/archives/cnsgc00004215-vol5-no4-eng.pdf

Congressional Record. (1967). Proceedings and debates of the 90th congress,
1st session, *113*(8). https://www.govinfo.gov/content/pkg/GPO-CRECB
-1967-pt8/pdf/GPO-CRECB-1967-pt8-3-1.pdf

Hansard Debates. (2000). Special committee to prevent the abuse and exploitation
of children through the sex trade. Legislative Assembly of Saskatchewan
Twenty-fourth Legislature.

Inco Metals Company. (1981). BLOCK PARENT: A place to turn in an
emergency. *Inco Triangle, 41*(5), 14–15. https://www.sudburymuseums.ca
/triangle/data/INCOTriangle-19810501.pdf

International Centre for the Prevention of Crime (ICPC). (2008). *Crime
prevention and community safety: Trends and perspectives.* https://cipc-icpc.org
/wp-content/uploads/2019/08/International_Report_on_Crime_Prevention
_and_Community_Safety_ANG.pdf

Minister of Supply and Services Canada. (1983). *The good neighbours crime
prevention handbook.* Solicitor General.

Milan, A. (2015, March 30). *Women in Canada: A Gender-Based Statistics Report.*
Statistics Canada. https://www150.statcan.gc.ca/n1/pub/89-503-x/2015001
/article/14152-eng.htm

Juvenile Delinquents Act, Canada SC 1908, c 40

Statistics Canada. (2021). *Volunteering counts: Formal and informal contributions
of Canadians 2018.* https://www150.statcan.gc.ca/n1/daily-quotidien
/210423/dq210423a-eng.htm

Statistics Canada. (2022). *The Canadian census: A rich portrait of the country's
religious and ethnocultural diversity.* https://www150.statcan.gc.ca/n1/daily
-quotidien/221026/dq221026b-eng.htm

UN Economic and Social Council (ECOSOC). (2002). *UN Economic and Social
Council Resolution 2002/13: Action to Promote Effective Crime Prevention,*
24 July 2002, E/RES/2002/13, https://www.refworld.org/docid
/46c455830.html

Index